Elizabeth W. (Elizabeth Williams) Champney, Elizabeth Williams
Champney

Three Vassar Girls in Italy

A Holiday Trip of Three College Girls Through Germany

Elizabeth W. (Elizabeth Williams) Champney, Elizabeth Williams Champney

Three Vassar Girls in Italy
A Holiday Trip of Three College Girls Through Germany

ISBN/EAN: 9783744760225

Printed in Europe, USA, Canada, Australia, Japan

Cover: Foto ©Thomas Meinert / pixelio.de

More available books at **www.hansebooks.com**

THREE VASSAR GIRLS

IN. ITALY.

A HOLIDAY EXCURSION OF THREE COLLEGE GIRLS

THROUGH THE CLASSIC LANDS.

BY

LIZZIE W. CHAMPNEY,

AUTHOR OF "A NEGLECTED CORNER OF EUROPE," "THREE VASSAR GIRLS ABROAD," ETC.

ILLUSTRATED BY "CHAMP,"

AND OTHER DISTINGUISHED ARTISTS.

BOSTON:
ESTES AND LAURIAT, PUBLISHERS,
301-305 WASHINGTON STREET.
1886.

CONTENTS.

LIST OF ILLUSTRATIONS.

THREE VASSAR GIRLS IN ITALY.

Three Vassar Girls in Italy.

CHAPTER I.

THE NORTH OF ITALY.

MILAN. — COMO. — VERONA.

HE was a Vassar Girl, and that decided it.

Aunt Pen had a prejudice against
women doctors, and an idea that the
entire profession wore divided skirts,
rode bicycles, cut their hair short, and
were spiritualistic trance mediums.

Please understand she *had* this
notion; for since we have known Doctor Victoria Delavan our minds
have suffered illumination.

Aunt Pen said to me privately after our first interview, " Phœbe,
she would hold her own with any of the old patroon families. I wish
you had half her dignity. She carries her head as if she were a
duchess."

We were not surprised when we learned afterward that she is an
heiress, and has taken up the study of medicine for the love of it, and
in the hope of doing good. It was Professor Schneidemuskel who told
us this, for Victoria seldom talks about herself. We really ought not
to call her "Doctor" yet, for she is only a medical student at Zurich,

and it will be some time before she obtains her degree, especially if she interrupts her course by trips like the present. But she does not seem in any haste to graduate. She says there is plenty of time; and I suppose she thinks that since the aim of all this study is to do good in the end, stopping to do it now is only so much clear gain. So when the Professor told her that there was a sick girl who needed to be taken to Italy for the winter and to have a regular course of treatment

VICTORIA.

from a companion who should know more about medicine than an ordinary nurse, she locked up her books and came to us. Aunt Pen took to her at once on account of her prepossessing manners; Uncle Jonah liked her sparkling good humor; and I saw in her a pillar of strength, she was so self-reliant and energetic. Uncle Jonah and Aunt Pen are the dearest and best people in the world, but I have to decide everything for them; and since I have become weak and nervous I have longed for some one to take the lead, say what must be done, and make me do it. Still, with all this in the favor of Doctor Victoria, I never could

have felt the absolute confidence in her which I do now if she had not happened to mention that she was a Vassar girl. Then I knew her through and through, for I am a Vassar girl myself, though I have only just completed my Freshman year, and ought not to boast of having the college stamp at all; but there is no bond among girls like the one of having been at Vassar. I suppose that possibly two veterans who had served under the first Napoleon might have something of the same feeling, but not exactly.

The winds that swept down from the Alps were becoming more and more glacial, and we left Zurich for Italy via Mont Cenis. It was a long, cold journey, and the account which Uncle Jonah read aloud of Napoleon crossing the Alps seemed to make it drearier and colder.

I was interested in the enterprise which has accomplished this piece of engineering, for the tunnel is the stupefaction of Europeans, many of whom predicted that it would never be finished. My Cousin Nat thinks he would rather have gone over the mountains with Napoleon; but the rest of our party prefer the present mode of travelling.

This reminds me that I have not mentioned Nat as yet. He is my cousin Nathaniel P. Willis Todd, aged fifteen, whom I am supposed to be preparing for college; though with all our sight-seeing the lessons are sadly interrupted, and he rarely gets more than two or three readings from Cæsar during the week. He mortally hates Latin; and says he wishes Brutus had assassinated Cæsar in his cradle, before he had time to write his " Gallic Wars."

NAT.

I suppose that Turin was really the first Italian city that we passed through, but our first stop was at this lovely city of

MILAN.

Our first view gave us the cathedral with its forest of pinnacles, each one tipped with a statue, — nearly eight thousand, they say, in all. Nat said it made him think of Resurrection Day to see this host of worthies standing on tiptoe between earth and heaven, — all noble characters who have walked in white and earned a white stone in a double sense. Perhaps it sounds irreverent, but I know Nat did not mean it so ; for when we went inside, the choir were chanting "Te Deum

Laudamus," and Nat whispered to me, "I told you so. Does n't it seem as if those marble men and women were singing, —

> 'The glorious company of the Apostles praise Thee,
> The goodly fellowship of the Prophets praise Thee,
> The noble army of Martyrs praise Thee'?"

Nat has his moments; but for all his mimicry and love of teasing, I shall always believe from that glimpse that he has a very tender heart.

Milan is so beautiful that I am sorry we are to stay here but a very few days. Victoria says it is hardly Italy yet; but it is interesting enough for me. Uncle Jonah has given me this large book in which to write my impressions, and has promised to buy photographs of the places which interest me, to paste opposite the written page; and I hope in this way to make a satisfactory record of our Italian winter.

I almost wish that I knew less of what is coming; the richness of the field oppresses me. I like Milan and would like to linger here a long time, for I feel as if I could contain what it has to give me; but all Italy! I turn to Mrs. Browning and read, —

> "'Now tell us what is Italy?' men ask;
> And others answer, 'Virgil, Cicero,
> Catullus, Cæsar.' 'What beside, to task
> The memory closer?' 'Why, Boccaccio,
> Dante, Petrarca, and if still the flask
> Appears to yield its wine by drops too slow,
> Angelo, Raphael, Pergolese, — all
> Whose strong hearts beat through stone, or charged again
> The paints with fire of souls electrical,
> Or broke up heaven for music.'"

This, too, is only a small part of what we are to expect. If I could only really *see* understandingly the things which I shall look at, this tour would be equal to a liberal education.

Nat is talking now with Victoria. "The Chevalier Bayard was killed near Milan, was he not, Miss Delavan?"

BAYARD.

" Yes, Nat; the Chevalier *sans peur et sans reproche* fought twice before the city. Once, in the beginning of the reign of Louis XII., he led the French forces into the city, where he was taken prisoner by Ludovico Sforza, surnamed, from his swarthy complexion, 'the Moor.' He was released, and for several years did honor to knighthood, showing all the virtues which Tennyson attributes to Sir Galahad. But Milan was also a city of doom for him, and he died fighting before it, on the 30th of April, 1524."

There is a little silence, and then Nat says, " Tell me more about him, Miss Delavan, please;" and Victoria answers, —

" With all his renown he was a very modest man. When Francis I. wished to be made a knight by Bayard on his first battlefield, the soldier thought himself unworthy to bestow this degree upon his sovereign. But when the king insisted, Bayard replied, 'Assuredly, Sire, I will do it, since it is your pleasure;' and taking his sword, he added, 'Avail it as much as if I were Roland or Oliver, Godfrey or his brother Baldwin.' Little thought the self-distrustful knight that his own name would one day shine brighter upon the pages of chivalry than those which seemed to him so illustrious! Who knows, Nat, but you may make a Bayard of yourself?"

" We don't have such chances nowadays; but tell me about his death."

" Francis I. was fighting in Italy against the forces of Charles V. of Spain, commanded by the traitor the Constable de Bourbon. Bayard had command of a small body of Frenchmen at the little village of Rebec near Milan, when the Spanish army came upon them and they were forced to retreat. Bayard was mortally wounded by a shot from an arquebuse, and was lifted from his saddle to the ground. A little company of his friends stood around him and the advance guard of the Spaniards came up, led by Bourbon, who paused, and, looking sadly down upon his old comrade, said, ' Bayard, my friend, I am sore distressed at your mishap. I will send in quest for the best surgeons in this country, and by God's help you will soon be healed.' But Bayard replied, 'My Lord, there is no pity for me. I die having done my duty; but I have pity for you, to see you serving against your king, your country, and your oath.'"

"Good for him! Did Bourbon kill him?"

"No; he turned away abashed, and commanded that a tent should be placed over him, and that everything should be done for him that was possible; but the good knight was so sorely wounded that he died in a few hours."

"What became of Bourbon after that?"

"We shall hear of him again at Rome. There is another French knight, a companion and friend of Bayard, though more nobly born and for a time commander of all the French forces in Italy, who is associated with Milan."

"Yes, I know,— Gaston de Foix; we saw his statue at the Archæological Museum the other day, and I grubbed up all I could about him. He was killed at the Battle of Ravenna after he had gained it and had carried on such a campaign that he won for himself the title of the 'Thunderbolt of Italy.' I have no doubt his exploits were just as brilliant or more so than Bayard's, but some way we all love the gentle knight best."

Victoria has actually succeeded in interesting Nat in history. I wonder whether she could do as much for Julius Cæsar. I am afraid not. All of those old Romans are so far back that we don't realize that they lived at all.

We have been to see Leonardo da Vinci's great picture, "The Last Supper," in the refectory of Santa Maria delle Grazie. I knew in advance that the painting was ruined, that the plaster had peeled off in parts, that an inundation had soaked away the colors, that the horses of the French soldiery stabled in the convent had kicked away the lower part of the picture, and that mould and restoration had done their worst to obliterate the masterpiece; and yet I was not quite

DEATH OF BAYARD.

prepared for the wreck which we were shown. My feeling was one of dumb rage and disappointment; for I had seen the copy in the Royal Academy in London, — a copy made two hundred years ago, — and I realized what a treasure the world has lost. I believe the tears really came into my eyes, for Aunt Pen turned upon me indignantly with, —

"Phœbe Todd, you don't mean to say that you see anything in that disgraceful old wall to make you cry! If it were mine, I would have it thoroughly cleaned and kalsomined; it's too shabby for anything! And how shameful in them to pretend that it is anything extraordinary!"

But while I looked, one part after another came out of the dimness; the design was there if not the coloring, and one could see the varying expressions of grief, horror, and indignation with which the different disciples ask, "Lord, is it I?"

Nat was anxious to verify the tipping over of the salt-cellar by Judas in his surprise, which has ever since been an ill omen; and he found the queer description of the picture in broken English of which Mark Twain speaks: "Peter argumenting in a threatening and angrily condition at Judas Iscariot." I have left a bunch of violets in front of the noble statue of Da Vinci in the Square. I am glad to have seen this great picture, and yet sorry, — it preaches such a pathetic sermon of decay. I do not see why noble and beautiful things should not last forever, and I said so to Victoria. She replied with a quotation: —

> "I read on the porch of a palace bold,
>   On a brazen tablet letters cast,
> 'A house, though a million winters old,
>   A house of earth comes down at last.'
> Then quarry thy rock from the crystal all,
> And build the dome which shall not fall."

COMO.

LAST night we saw Don Giovanni at La Scala Theatre at Milan; to-day we are looking across the lake at a scene for all the world like a theatrical drop-curtain. The water has that unnatural blue, the white villas are arranged for effect, even the dusty gray foliage of the olives and the dark greens of the walnuts are interspersed with an eye to contrast, and the row-boats go drifting by, — now merrily to the sound of gay music, and now languidly as in a dream. The mountains about the lake are much higher and steeper than I had imagined. There would not seem to be level space enough anywhere for a village; but villages and even towns there are, which cut terraces for themselves or cling to the face of the cliffs. We saw them as we steamed around to Lecco at the head of the other arm of the lake. The white houses looked very picturesque, rising one above the other like the tiers of seats in an amphitheatre, but they must be very uncomfortable towns to live in. Aunt Pen said it reminded her of Kansas City; but I do not think any of the rest of us were struck with the resemblance.

We stopped on the way at Bellaggio, famed for its beautiful villas. We had the privilege of gazing from the outside at the Villa Giulia, owned by the King of the Belgians, to which visitors are not admitted, and of looking at a gallery of pictures belonging to a more hospitably inclined though less exalted personage.

Here at Lecco we are staying at an inn called "Il Croce di Malta," —the Maltese Cross. Nat says the name is a swindle, for he has not been able to discover anything Maltese about the place, not even a cat.

VERONA.

POOR Nat has had a severe disappointment. He wanted to visit Cremona and buy a violin there. I do not suppose that he really

GASTON DE FOIX.

expected to find one made by the Amati or the Stradivari, for the
first family ceased to manufacture violins in 1620, and the latter in
1728. But these celebrated manufacturers have shed such a lustre
on their native city, that to have a genuine Cremona violin, be it of
the ordinary factory kind, would have a distinguished sound. However, Cremona lies too far to the southward to be directly on our route
to Venice; and so here we are at Verona with a very cross boy who
will not be consoled for the loss of his fiddle. The city is a beautiful
one, with stately palaces, one of which, with barred lower windows
and a long balcony, I was sure was Juliet's home. I could imagine
her leaning over the balustrade and talking with Romeo below. To
be sure, the balcony jutted upon the street and not upon a garden;
but then, the garden might have been there in Capulet's time. I felt
so certain that I had discovered the home of the Capulets by a sort
of presentiment, that I asked a little man at the door the name of the
building only to find that it was the Palazzo Bevilacqua, and that
the Capulets had much humbler quarters in an unimpressive house
opening upon a stable court. The guide-book says that it is now an
inn, and I had asked Uncle Jonah to take rooms there; but when I
saw the place I decided that no amount of sentiment could make
me wish to lodge there. I thought we must have mistaken our way,
but our guide showed us the cap (the emblem of the family) carved
in stone over the great gateway. It is interesting to me to know
what these noble names mean. The de la Scala, whose beautiful
tombs we have visited, derive their name from the word ladder; and
ladders were intertwined in the iron tracery that surrounded them.
Nat was sure that they had something to do with a hook-and-ladder
company; and, indeed, the insignia of a bishop of that family, com-
bined as the ladder was with a crosier and mitre, the latter looking
a good deal like a fireman's helmet, might have made a very appropriate decoration over an engine-house door. The de la Scala seem
to have been noble clear through, and not banditti veneered with a

pretence of nobility, like the Sforzas of Milan. Two of this family were patrons of Dante, — Can Grande, or the great dog (and one wonders why he bore such a name), and Bartolomeo, who is supposed to be the Escalus Prince of Verona whom Shakspeare mentions.

We had a comical guide, who took us to see Juliet's tomb, and who spoke the drollest broken English.

"Theese," said he, pointing to the sarcophagus, "is the spot where the lovely Juliet was *gravied*."

We all looked blank enough; and Aunt Pen exclaimed, "Dear me! you don't mean to say that she was cooked in that stone dish by cannibals!"

Then it was the guide's turn to be puzzled, and to spread his hands and explain, —

"No, Signora, not Anibal, Romeo; Juliet was gravied, — what you call him? — entombed, buried, — Juliet, the sweetheart of Romeo, of Shakspeare."

"The sweetheart of Shakspeare, you unconscionable man!" Uncle Jonah exclaimed. "Ann Hathaway was Shakspeare's sweetheart. We saw her grave in England. This I understand you to represent as the tomb of Juliet Capulet; don't mix things, and make your story any more improbable than it is. I have seen Romeo and Juliet repeatedly on the stage, and the tomb was not at all like this base fabrication. Why, man! how could Juliet and the County Paris and Romeo and a lighted lantern, not to mention the skulls and bones of the dead-and-gone Capulets, all cram themselves into that water-trough? It 's more than absurd; it 's preposterous!" And with an angry sniff Uncle Jonah turned indignantly away.

The poor guide was so depressed that Victoria had to apologize for Shakspeare in order to cheer him up, and said that she believed the great dramatist had never been in Verona, or he would have drawn his scenes nearer to nature. The little man brightened, and said that Shakspeare was a great man. Some English tourists had

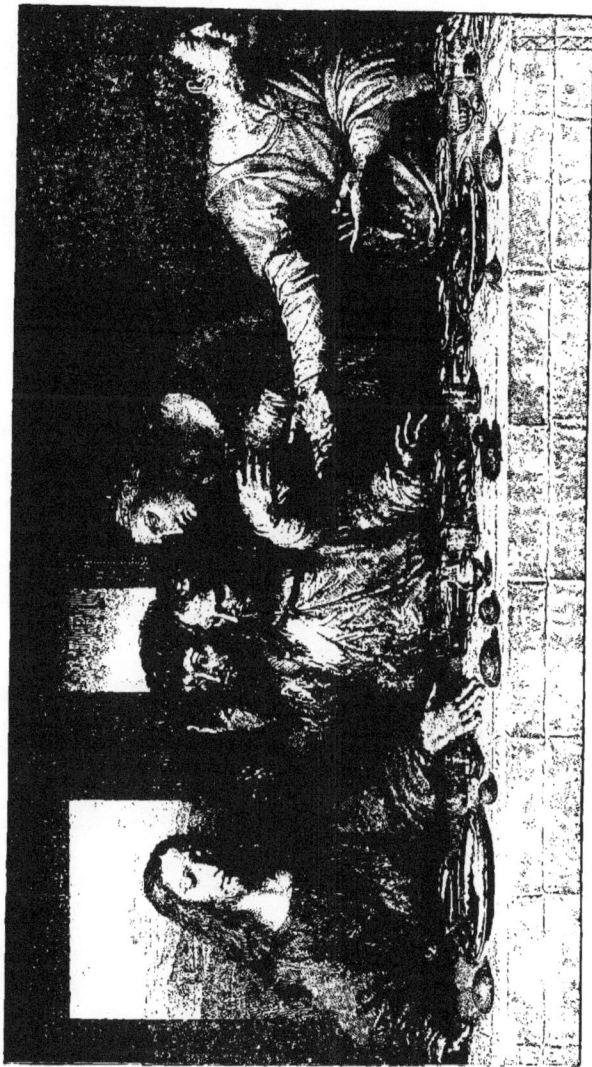

LAST SUPPER. — LEONARDO DA VINCI.

given him a copy of " Romeo and Juliet," and he had committed a part of the play to memory. Would we like to hear him rehearse? His speaking had usually great impression upon " ze English." Aunt and Uncle had gone; but of course Nat and I wanted to hear him, and Victoria lingered, to please us.

I cannot give his gestures, and they were the most comical part. He said that he had always felt that he had a talent for the stage, and had acted in the church miracle-plays when a boy. His favorite accompaniment to every line was to point jerkingly at the sky. He did not seem offended that we laughed, while he spoke, until the tears ran down our cheeks. Perhaps the tears atoned for the laughter, and he regarded it as merely hysterical. His elocution made such "great impression" upon Nat that he quite rolled over into Juliet's tomb. The part chosen was Romeo's soliloquy in Capulet's garden; he ran on something like this : —

THE GUIDE.

> " But, sofe ! what light tru yonder vindow bricks ?
> It ees ze yeast, and Juliet ees ze sone !
> Arise, fair soné, onde keel ze enfious mun,
> Oo ees olready seek onde pell wiz grief,
> Zat zou her med art far more fear zan she.
> .   .   .   .
> She spiks, yet she say nossing : wot of zat?
> Her heye de corset ; I vill answer eet.
> I ame too boulde, 't is not to me she spik :
> Two of ze fairy star in all ze heffen
> Hafing some pizness do hentreat her heyes
> To zwinkle in zere — to zwinkle — in vat you call em'? "

And as we from stress of too much emotion were quite unable to prompt him, he broke down utterly.

He tried again, with Romeo's speech before he drinks the poison. This, he informed us, as it takes place at Juliet's tomb, the Englishman who gave him the book had told him might come in very well in his duty as showman. Perhaps the donor of the book had given him some lessons, for he invariably prefixed a Cockney *h* to *eyes* and a few other words.

This selection proved so extremely harrowing, that Nat remained in the sarcophagus, where he could give vent to his emotion by tumbling and kicking unseen. The guide began by rolling his eyes horribly and stretching out his arms toward Victoria, who immediately retreated into the monastery as he cried, —

> " Heyes, look your last !
> Harms, tek your last embraze !"

At the close of his speech he drew from his pocket a flask which I imagine contained something stronger than Veronese wine, and with a long draught which, had it been poison, must have been sufficient to kill ten Romeos, exclaimed, —

> " Thus with a keese I die ! "

and sank impressively back into the sarcophagus, greatly to the surprise of Nat, who had not expected this ending, and had no mind to enact Juliet to such a heavy Romeo.

I ought not to have given so much space to this comical incident; for now I have no time to tell of our visit to the amphitheatre, erected, it is supposed, by Diocletian, — a great circus five hundred by four hundred feet, with dens for wild beasts, and an aqueduct for flooding the arena for naval battles. I would like to write something of the church of San Zenone, too, built in the exuberant Italian Gothic; but other churches clamor for notice, for Verona is a thing of the past, and we are now in Venice.

PALAZZO BEVILACQUA.

CHAPTER II.

I was sure that I would be disappointed in Venice. I knew before-hand that it was one of those exaggerated and too much painted and written-up places which never hold their own with their reputation. But the moment we left the railroad station and entered a gondola we were in fairy-land. It was night, and there were the reflections of the lights in the canals, and the gondoliers and the tall mysterious palaces, the cupola of St. Mark's silhouetted against the moonlit sky, the wild cries and snatches of Italian songs, — the Venice of Byron and the painters. I think I was in a kind of trance until some one asked if I remembered the remark of the travelled fool, who, being asked how he liked Venice, replied that really he ought not to express an opinion, since there must have been an inundation prior to his arrival, for the city was under water during his entire stay! The others are off sight-seeing to-day, but Verona tired me so, that they think I had better not attempt much gadding abroad as yet. So Victoria has pulled my couch to the window, and made me comfortable with wraps and guide-books and a tiny silver bell with which I can summon our Venetian maid Luisa when I want her.

Just at present I do not wish her. I would rather lie here and write up my journal and paste in the photographs. Here is one from an altar-piece by one of the old masters which represents angels play-ing on triangles, bass-viols, banjos, and violins. It is a little startling to us who are accustomed to think of the harp as the only heavenly

3

instrument. But after all I don't see why angels, if they play at all, should not have the best; and the harp alone is not comparable to a full orchestra. Here in Italy all these worldly instruments are used in church choirs with very noble effect. But I think, on the whole, I 'll not use that photograph, for it irritates Nat, reminding him of his lost fiddle. But this has nothing to do with Venice. And first I ought to describe our surroundings. We have taken apartments on the third floor of a palace, a princely but rather desolate building which they say was occupied long ago by one of the doges, or dukes, of Venice. The rooms are very high and chilly. This one has a tessellated marble floor, and a frescoed ceiling said to have been painted by one of Titian's pupils. The staircase is a very grand affair, entirely of white marble slabs, with a balustrade of gilded metal-work, the newel imitated from the base of one of the flag-masts in front of St. Mark's. Among other allegorical emblems I noticed that it bore representations of the winged lion of St. Mark. There is a balcony before my window, and across the narrow canal there looms another palace grander than this, with corridors on the second story open to the air, the story above supported by fluted pillars with beautiful arches, the spaces between the mouldings forming dark quatre-foils, and sharp triangles such as Ruskin describes in his " Stones of Venice." I am more interested in people than in architecture, and I wish I knew just which doge lived in this house, and the history of the artist who painted the ceiling. Perhaps the old doge had a daughter, and the artist fell in love with her, as they say Titian fell in love with Palma's daughter; and perhaps while her father in his horned cap was going through the ceremony of marrying the Adriatic by casting into it from the ship " Bucentaur " a ring blessed by the Pope, the lovely Tessa, or Violante, or Cecilia stole down the marble staircase and eloped with the artist. But the doge could only have lived here before his election, for while he held the chief dignity he must have occupied the doges' palace; and I do not envy him his life there under the watch of the grim Council of Ten,

FOOT OF FLAGSTAFF.

who could at any moment send him across the Bridge of Sighs to his death. Dear me, what romantic nonsense I am writing! I had quite forgotten for the moment that Mr. Howells calls the Bridge of Sighs a " pathetic swindle,".proves that it was not built till the end of the sixteenth century, and that no political offend-
ers, but simply common criminals, went over it from their trial to prison.

I can see a gentleman walking within the arcades of the palace op-posite. He is evidently an Italian, and has the bearing of a noble; but then they all have that. Our gondo-lier last night might have been a de-scendant of the Foscari.

I cannot see the water from where I lie, but Nat says that the palace steps opposite descend beneath it, and there is a row of green-and-white hitching-posts for gondolas in front of it. He said they looked like stalks of asparagus.

UNCLE JONAH.

Nat is a great tease, like most boys of his age, and likes nothing better than to excite interest in some particular subject and then, while pretending to give information, to go all around Robin Hood's barn talking in the most provoking manner of things about which one does not in the least care to hear. But in the main he is a good-natured boy. Uncle Jonah must have been like him in his youth, for he is as droll as droll can be. You will know my Uncle Jonah, if you ever see him, by his cherub wings. He is quite bald, with the exception of two little flame-shaped locks which remind one of the wings on Mercury's cap. When Uncle Jonah is excited, these locks bristle electrically; when he is ill or tired, they droop, lose their flamboyant character, and are only little meshes of gray hair.

Aunt Pen is a well-preserved, good-natured, rather worldly-minded, ponderous woman. You have seen her often, shopping on Broadway and lunching at Purcell's. She is very fond of his Bath buns, and often makes extensive shopping excursions just as an excuse for dropping in at Purcell's for a cup of coffee. She always wears black satin dresses which fit as if she had been poured into them, with more or less jet trimming according to the occasion, and an immense seal-skin cloak in nearly all weathers. She is fond of pets, and Uncle Jonah or the maid or Nat has to carry her menagerie, which consists just now of two dogs, a pug and a skye, which are insanely jealous of each other; some very accomplished canaries that we bought in Geneva, and an Angora cat from Paris, with a tail like the plume of Henri of Navarre, — by the way, that is

AUNT PEN.

what we call him. She wanted to buy some educated fleas; but Uncle Jonah mutinied, and she gave up the project. I am one of her pets. She told mother that I was killing myself with study at Vassar and must go abroad. I had gained twenty pounds and could not get into any of my old dresses. Aunt Pen was sure that I had contracted dropsy of the heart, and mother became anxious and let her take me to Paris, stipulating only that I was not on any account to be married to a foreign count. So far, we have not met one who was marriageable; but my winter at Paris, with the dresses made by Monsieur le Mort, brought down my figure very satisfactorily to Aunt Pen. Some way, I could not stand

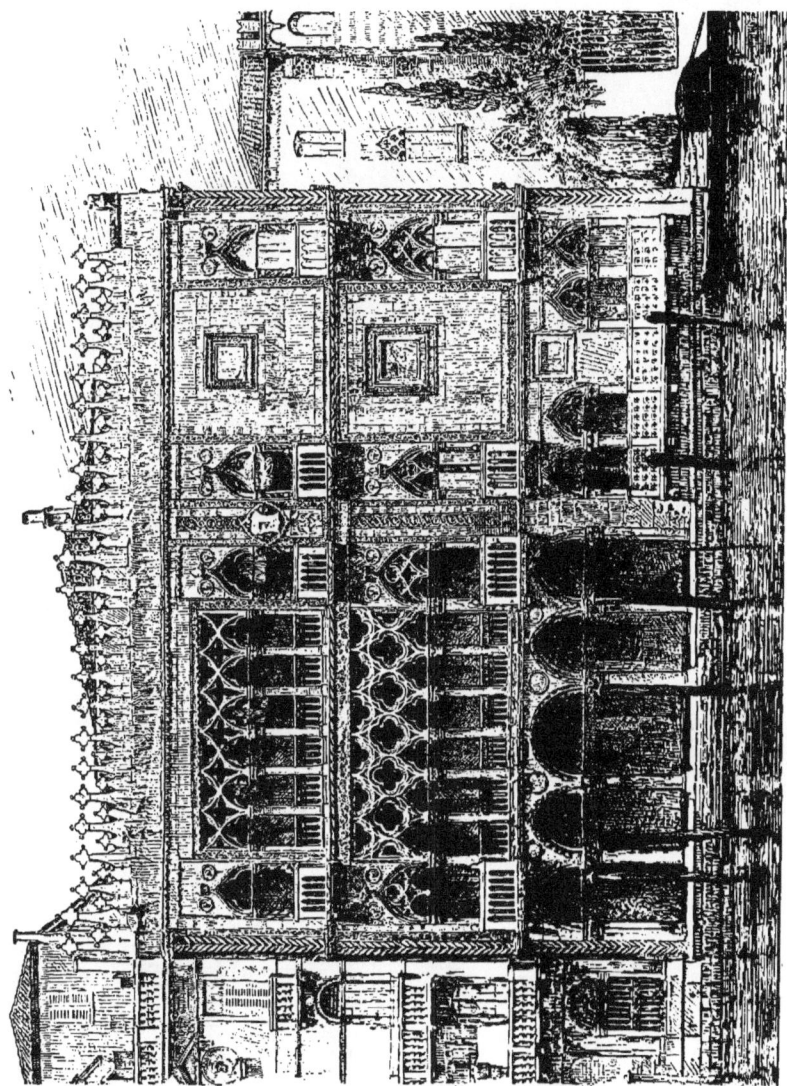

CA D'ORO.

the long walks that I did at home, and when I attempted to climb the Righi last summer I gave out when only a third of the way; and at Zurich I caught a dreadful cold, and the doctors say I must take care of myself. Aunt Pen thinks it is hearing Nat's Latin; but Doctor Victoria has different ideas on the subject, and has had all the Paris costumes folded away, has purchased soft flannels and had some very pretty wrappers and loose travelling suits made for me which are twice as becoming as the Le Mort dresses.

Aunt Pen is coming back now; I can hear her wheeze as she mounts the staircase. She fully expected to find elevators in Venice, and is indignant that there are none to be found. Doctor Victoria has come in with her. Aunt Pen always tires out in any excursion before the rest of the party, and has to be brought home. But I am glad Victoria has come; and now she shall sit beside me and tell me all she has seen, and I will jot it down as she talks. In this way I mean to profit by the eyes and feet of all the family.

CHAPTER III.

"What have I seen? Oh, Phœbe, how can I tell you! You must see it all yourself, for no description can give a picture of the Piazza of St. Mark, with its beautiful buildings, the shipping in the basin, the blue of the sky and the lagoon, and the changing panorama of the people. You shall go to-morrow if the weather is fine, for really the glorious sunshine makes out-of-doors warmer than this chilly interior."

"Indeed, Victoria," I reply, "I have not been really comfortable all the morning. That little German stove of white porcelain might thaw the atmosphere of a small room, but it makes no impression whatever in this great hall."

"I will have Luisa bring you a scaldino; but first let us have a good game of 'peas porridge hot.' Exercise is better than artificial heat."

"Certainly; but while we are cuffing each other, tell me about St. Mark's, and I will compare impressions to-morrow."

"You must not stay there long, for all the churches are mortally cold, and at St. Mark's you are liable to forget it, for it is the most bewitching church I was ever in, — the most sympathetic, I mean. The arches are not lofty; the roof seems to brood over you like the sense of God's love; there is no gaudy display of tinsel and gilding; the mosaics are very rich, but harmonious and unostentatious, and the color is subdued and mysterious. Little twinkling lamps, suspended by gilt chains, glimmer here and there through colored glasses. The music is distant and sweet; you see the incense curling as well as inhale it. It is the most poetic, dreamy place imaginable."

"Your description is very enthusiastic; but I don't seem to have any definite idea of how the church looks. I know it is not Gothic but Byzantine, and that it is built in the form of a Greek cross, but that is all."

"You saw the domes last night. There are five of them, each surmounted with a smaller onion-shaped one, and that by a jewelled weather-cock. Between the domes shoot airy pinnacles, enclosing statues, which, with the domes, add to the Eastern appearance of the building. The façade is very richly ornamented, and flocks of pigeons nestle in the cornices and flutter down to the pavement, to be fed by a pretty Venetian girl."

"Yes, I know," I interrupted; "one sees them always in pictures of Venice. I wonder why it is that the Venetians are so fond of doves."

PIGEONS OF ST. MARK'S.

"There is a legend," Victoria explained, "that when Admiral Dandolo was besieging Candia in the early part of the thirteenth century, he received information from the island by means of carrier pigeons which enabled him to take the fortress. He sent these birds to Venice with the news of his victory, and they and their

broods have been kept in the Piazza at the public expense ever since."

Aunt Pen knitted her brows thoughtfully. " I don't believe that story," she remarked at length, with an air of profound conviction. "Whoever heard of pigeons living five hundred years!"

I laughed; but Victoria explained that these were the descendants of the Dandolo pigeons. Aunt brightened. " If that is true," she said, " I must have a pair of them to take to America. No; I think I will send over a cage of them to your mother. She writes so many letters, they would be quite a saving in the way of postage."

It was a long time before I could persuade her that the journey across the ocean might be too much for even the original Dandolo pigeons, and the information seemed to dampen her interest in every-thing she had seen that day; for she declared that she did not think much of St. Mark's. She was rather disappointed in it, to tell the truth; for the acoustic properties were not good, and in point of rich-ness it could not at all compare with the new opera-house at Paris. She confessed, however, that the Piazza was very pretty; but why they should call it a Piazza, when it was no more like a veranda than Boston Common, but entirely unroofed and open to the sunlight, quite passed her comprehension. Victoria explained that *piazza* was the Italian word for square or place, and Aunt Pen dropped the sub-ject to inveigh against Italian cooking. She had not tasted it during her promenade, but she protested that all outdoors was perfumed with the scent of it. They were frying onions in the court below, and just beyond there was a cook-shop almost impossible to pass for the fumes of garlicky soup which issued from the door. The sight of clotted blood sold by the cupful made her sick; and how any one not in the last stages of famine could eat boiled snails, was beyond explanation!

Uncle Jonah and Nat had stopped at a café for luncheon, but she could not be induced to set foot inside the establishment. To be

SCIOLLO AND COLLEONI.

sure the slender repast which Luisa now served us, of croquettes mysteriously compounded, with a dessert of fruit and black coffee, was Italian in substance and preparation; but then we did not know too much of the secrets of our own kitchen.

Nat burst in upon us soon after lunch: "Oh, Cousin Phœbe, you ought to have been with us! We've made the acquaintance of a prince!"

"Really! Who is he?"

"I don't know. Father has his card, — Il Dottore Arlechino Facanapa — oh, no! those are the characters in the puppet-show we saw on the Piazza. A regular theatre of marionettes; beats Punch and Judy all to pieces! I mean to buy the play, translate it, and make myself a set of the puppets, if you will help me."

"That means, if I will translate the play and make the puppets, you will work them. Thank you! We will finish the First Book of Cæsar first. But what about the Prince?"

"Well, Phœbe, he was too ricochet for anything." (Nat meant *recherché.*) "We saw him walking in front of the Ducal Palace and we knew he was a Gran' Signor something or other. He came into the *café* just after us. I was choking with laughter at a poor German who was studying the bill of fare, trying in vain to understand the name of a single dish; but my merriment subsided, I can tell you, when I found father was in the same boat. Well, when the Prince noticed our perplexity, he came up and offered his services in English, with the prettiest air in the world, just like Facanapa in the puppet-show. You see there are strings that come down from the ceiling that jerk the left leg out, so. It makes a regular Beau Brummel bow."

"Nathaniel Willis Todd! what do you mean? Strings from the ceiling that jerked the Count's leg! You must be thinking of the torture-chambers of the Inquisition."

"Who said anything about the Count's legs? I was describing

the way in which the puppets are worked. There! don't look so like a martyr, and I'll go on. Father offered him a seat at our table and let him order the lunch. It was Number One! but did n't it cost, though? By the way, he is n't quite a prince, though he has the air of one; his card bore a crest, and — yes, this time in earnest — what

"STUDYING THE BILL OF FARE."

it said was, ' Co. Prospero Torlonia.' The 'Co.' stands for Conte, you know. Father told him that he had a letter to the Banker Tolonia at Rome, and asked him if he was related to him; and he said that was another branch of his family, that had gone into trade and disgraced the escutcheon. I should think the banker's millions might wash out the disgrace; but the Prince, I mean the Conte, did not seem to feel so."

"Does he live in Venice?"

"No; in Sicily somewhere. He is going to Rome next week; and when father said that we should, too, he hoped the acquaintance might be continued. He was almost too elegant, in his velvet coat and kid gloves; I could n't help feeling that people must think that father was his butler and that I was a groom. He had a way of thrusting one hand inside the breast of his coat and holding the other arm behind him, which was tremendously statuesque. When in Venice, he lives — "

"I know; don't tell me. He lives in the palace just across the canal."

LIBRARY OF ST. MARK'S.

" How did you know ? "

" I saw him walking just behind the arches. I recognized your description at once. To think the only time that a real live count has noticed our party I should have been cooped up at home ! "

" You will have plenty of chances; he is going to take us to-morrow to see the pictures at the Accademia."

" What condescension ! I am so overpowered by it that I fear I shall not be able to go."

" You must. He said that we were the first Americans he had ever met, though he has been in England. He remarked, too, that he had heard a great deal about American young ladies, and was curious to see what they are like."

" Then he must meet Victoria; she is altogether a better specimen of the genus than I am."

Nat continued his chatter. " And oh, Phœbe ! did Miss Delavan tell you about the pigeons ? How they came to Venice, I mean. They would be a good subject for a poem, now would n't they ? Put in plenty of bursting shot and shell, riddled banners, and broken masts, and I 'll speak it at the Academy. Then you can do the love-sick-maiden business. She might be a Christian captive in love with old Dandolo; and she could send him a lock of her hair along with a map of the fortress. But don't overdo that part, or you 'll make it too heavy."

" Yes; I think that a carrier pigeon who had to struggle along with a military map and too much maiden-hair might find himself pretty heavily handicapped."

" Good for you, Phœbe ! Leave out the maiden altogether; only I thought you might like to have her leaning on the parapets, looking away over the blue Ægean,— by the way, that was just what that Vassar girl was doing that we saw to-day—"

" Vassar girl ! Another ! When and where did you see her ? How do you know that she was —"

" Now, Cousin Phœbe, is n't that catechism about long enough?
We had gone around the Piazza to see the two Vulcans strike the
hours on a bell over the clock-tower. And did you know that the
face is divided after the old Italian fashion into twenty-four hours
instead of twelve? "

" Well, well, what of it? Tell me about the Vassar girl."

" My dear little cousin, don't get excited! I am answering your
questions in their regular order. You asked me *when* I saw her. By
the clock in the Piazza, it was exactly twenty minutes past seventeen
o'clock. She was standing in front of the statue of Bartolomeo Colleoni,
staring up at it, with just the air of admiration with which the lovesick
captive looked across the blue Ægean at old Dandolo. By the way,
did you know that that is considered one of the finest equestrian
statues in existence? "

" I don't care a fig for equestrian statues! I want to know about
her. Who was she? "

" Oh, come now! I have n't finished the original catechism. How
did I know she was a Vassar girl? In the first place, she was so
uncommonly homely — "

" Now, Nat, I suppose you mean to say that Victoria and I are
hideous! Very complimentary in you, I am sure! "

" My dear Phœbe, you were not at Vassar long enough to succumb
to the chilling blight of the place, and Miss Delavan is such a startling exception that I have all along had my doubts about her being
a Vassar girl at all. In the case of this young woman there was not
the least doubt of it. She wore glasses, but she took them off to look
at the statue, and she was so absorbed in her contemplations that
she did not notice that we were all three staring at her. Now, who
but a Vassar girl would be so taken up with a bronze or stone man
as not to notice three living ones? "

" Two and a half, you mean, Nat; be accurate, my dear boy."

" Phœbe, if you wish to hear the end of this adventure, don't indulge in sarcasm; it confuses my ideas and interrupts the flow of the narrative. After she had stared at old Colleoni awhile, she went around in front of the Library where the two granite columns are, one of which bears the Winged Lion of St. Mark, and the other, St. Theodore on a crocodile. You know St. Theodore was the patron of Venice before St. Mark, and he seems now to be the special patron of the gondoliers; at any rate, they make his column their favorite lounging-place. Come to think of it, I believe the gondola was modelled on the plan of the crocodile."

"Nathaniel Todd, don't tease me any more! You see how anxious I am to hear about her; perhaps she is some one whom I already know."

"Ain't I telling you every detail? How ungrateful you are! She gazed at the two pillars with the same fixidity, but not for so long a time, for the

"SHE GAZED AT THE COUNT CALMLY."

gondoliers beheld in her their natural prey, and they sprang upon and would doubtless have torn her in pieces and carried her home in twenty different gondolas, if we had not rescued her and taken her to her hotel, which was quite near."

"Did n't you ascertain her name?"

"No, my dear; it is a characteristic of Vassar girls that they don't confide their names to three unknown gentlemen, even when they owe their lives to them."

" Then tell me once for all how you knew she was a Vassar girl."

" She had that air, Phœbe, — that nameless something. She gazed at the Count calmly, not in the least impressed by his impressiveness. You will find that I am right, for we are bound to see her again."

" What did she talk about on her way to the hotel ? "

" Venice, of course, and statues; her heart is as stony as the nether millstone, and she is only interested in stone men. There are a good many sculptures at the Accademia; perhaps we shall see her there to-morrow."

CHAPTER IV.

WE have returned from the Academy. I have had a nap, and feel somewhat rested. Aunt Pen does not care a great deal for picture galleries. She found the Louvre a weariness of the flesh, and stipulated, when we talked of coming to Italy, that she should not be asked to admire pictures; and when the Count was announced, Victoria produced a stupid-looking volume on the nervous system, and declined to go. So we formed a party of four, — Uncle Jonah, the Count, Nat, and I. We took a gondola to the Riva dei Schiavoni, and walked along it to the Piazza. Then I saw for the first time what Victoria had described, — the palaces and the façade of St. Mark's, with the bronze horses that have had such a wonderful history. If they could only talk as animals and statues do in fairy stories, they would tell us of how they once stood on Nero's triumphal arch and then on Trajan's, in old Rome, having been made for the Emperor by some Greek artist whose name is unknown now, though they are so beautiful that it was imagined they might be the work of Lysippus. Next, Constantine took them to Constantinople, and,

> " With eyes as bright as Phosphorus,
> They glared upon the Bosphorus,"

until Doge Dandolo, that fierce old fighter, won them from the Turk and brought them to Venice in 1204. After that it took no less a jockey than Napoleon to drive this remarkable four-in-hand to Paris, where they pawed the air impatiently for eighteen years over the triumphal arch in the Place de Carrousel, at the end of which period, with snorting nostrils and flowing manes, they galloped gladly back to Venice, and took up their stations again over the portals of the great cathedral.

We did not go inside, but went directly to the Academy of Fine Arts, which is devoted almost exclusively to painters of the Venetian

"COPYING THE MASTERPIECES."

School,— Titian, Paul Veronese, Tintoretto, the two Palmas, Pordenone, and Giorgione. Artists were busy here and there, copying the old masterpieces in fresher colors. I was glad the Count was with us, for he seemed to know something of art, and explained the paintings. As I had formed no opinion of my own, I could only take refuge behind Ruskin; and I found, after examining the masterpieces, that I

THE ASSUMPTION.

did not entirely agree with him. I was told that the " Presentation of the Virgin at the Temple," by Titian, is considered the finest picture in the Academy; but I stood longer before his " Assumption," which is altogether wonderful. The Virgin is borne upward by myriads of cherub children as buoyant as so many little balloons. You can almost feel the rush of wind as they impel her upward, away from the pathetic reaching arms which stretch after her in vain. Mary's face and attitude are ecstatic. Titian has given us a mere symbol of what she sees, — a representation of Divine Love brooding over her, and angels bringing her crown; but we know that Mary sees even more than this, for all heaven is reflected in her rapt gaze. I looked at the picture so long, that I forgot the place and my companions. When I came out of my vision the others were talking about Titian. Nat was jotting down in his note-book the fact that he was born in 1477, a little after Michael Angelo, and before Raphael, at Cadore, a village in the wild mountains. I knew that he studied under Bellini and Palma, and that Giorgione was his rival at first, and Pordenone later on, when both painted in the Council Hall; but I had never heard the story of his beautiful domestic life as the Count told it to us. He lived near the Church of the Jesuits, just aside from the Fondamente Nuove, in a house which he made more and more beautiful as wealth came to him. But his loved wife Cecilia died when he was in middle life, leaving him with three little children, Pomponio, Orazio, and Lavinia; and after that, art was his only joy. He sent to Cadore for his sister Orsa, who came to him and took Cecilia's place as guardian of his children. Lavinia grew up into a superb beauty, as we know from the many pictures of her which her father has handed down, — especially the one in the Berlin Museum, which represents her in a yellow silk dress, with a jewelled diadem, necklace, and girdle, supporting with both hands a silver dish filled with fruit and flowers. Titian's house had a beautiful garden stretching down to the water's edge, and in this garden it is said he was fond of entertaining very good company. I can fancy what it looked like, with the table spread under the shade of the vines, and the poet Ariosto, Titian's friend, dictating sonnets for Lavinia to sing to the organ which her father purchased for her, and Aretino, the sculptor and scholar, helping Pomponio with his Latin.

A curious letter of Aretino to the little Pomponio still exists.

" Pomponio Monsignorino," he writes to the little boy who is away with his relatives in the wild mountains of Cadore, " it is time that you should return from the country, where there is no school. So come; and now that you are twelve years old, you shall write some exercises in Hebrew, in Greek, and in Latin, that will astonish the doctors, as the pictures astonish the artists of Italy, which are painted by Messer, your father. So no more, but keep yourself warm and in good appetite."

It is a pity that Pomponio grew up a dissolute fellow, disgracing the priest's habit which he assumed. But Orazio and Lavinia were the comfort of their father's old age. At seventy, Titian painted incessantly; besides his great masterpieces, finding time for portraits of many of the eminent men of his time, while nearly all the monarchs of the period were his patrons. At seventy-seven he went to Rome to study Michael Angelo's method, and at ninety-nine he said that he was only beginning to learn the art of painting. That was the year that he died of the plague, still actively engaged in work, with his natural force unabated, as was proved by his last picture, " The Entombment," finished the year he died. We are going sometime to the Frari, or Church of the Franciscans, to see his tomb.

We looked at a great many other pictures; but Titian is surely the king of the Venetian School. Nat was right in his belief that we would meet the unknown, supposititious Vassar girl at the Academy. While we were admiring " The Entombment," he gently jogged my elbow and remarked, " There, was n't I right? Is n't she a fright, though ? "

" Who ? " I asked, — " Mary ? " thinking that possibly he referred to one of the personages in the pictures.

FEAST AT THE HOUSE OF LEVI.

" Hush!" said Nat; "the unknown beauty from Vassar."

Really, the girl was painfully plain, tall and ungainly, with a high forehead, from which the hair was brushed back in an uncompromising, don't-care way, which seemed to say, "I know I am homely, and there is no use disguising the matter; so there!"

Uncle Jonah bowed to her, and her face lit up with such pleasant and grateful recognition, that he brought me forward, saying, "Allow me to present my niece, Miss Phœbe Todd."

The girl held out her hand frankly. "I have noticed you," she said. "You seem to like Titian."

From that we drifted into conversation about the Venetian painters, and I told her that I could not quite comprehend Ruskin's enthusiasm for Giorgione, but I could see that Tintoretto was a great colorist, though no doubt an artist could more fully appreciate the grand harmony of his rich, low-toned pictures. I thought that she must be an artist; and so she was, but not a painter. She told us that she was trying to be a sculptor, and had a little studio in Rome, but that she had come to Venice to make a portrait bust of the baby boy of a certain Mrs. Richlands,

MRS. RICHLANDS.

a European American who has given up her native land, and roams about from city to city in what seems to me a very desolate and homeless way. Our new acquaintance said that her patroness was in the next room, and asked permission to introduce her, as she was always glad to meet compatriots. Then she ran away and brought her in, — a stylish woman, with a worldly manner and a self-satisfied smile; but her speech was kinder than her looks, for she was very polite to us all, and especially to me. For all that Nat had said of the unprepossessing appearance of the supposed Vassar girl, he was really interested in her, and they were soon talking together quite freely. I heard him say that his favorite painter was Paul Veronese; and I was rather ashamed of Nat's taste, for Veronese delights in rather gaudy color, bright reds, yellows, and blues, and he takes a special pleasure in depicting people eating. Some one has said, that to tell a story that will amuse children, you must put a great deal of dinner-party in it. It seems to me that many grown people have not advanced beyond that stage, and I said so.

Nat was a little nettled. " I am sure, Cousin Phœbe," he said, " that you like a party better than anything else, and I do not see that a party without a dinner is so very superior to a party with one."

Mrs. Richlands laughed, and said Nat had the right idea, and that we must all come to her receptions, for she always began them with a supper; people were so much more amiable after a good meal. The Count paid very particular attention, and I could see that he meant to avail himself of the invitation; but Nat's friend explained that Veronese had orders to paint four great feasts for different convent refectories. One of these pictures, " The Marriage of Cana," we saw at the Louvre; and here we found another of these famous banquets, " The Feast in the House of Levi." As we stood before it I asked Nat to explain, if he could, why he liked it, and he ran on something in this style: —

" Why, you see, it is so downright jolly and real, and every one seems to be having such a good time. There is an abundance to eat and drink; even the servants are stowing away their share. The men-at-arms on the staircase are stuffing themselves, the children have eaten all they want, and even the dog has a well-fed, lazy air. Just look at that plate of food that the old party is cutting up for Christ! No wonder the Pharisees called him gluttonous, if they saw that dish. And Levi is scolding the butler for not bringing up more wine.

I can hear him now, ' Go to, Sirrah! Hast thou not heard that at the marriage of Cana there were six water-pots of wine, containing two or three firkins apiece? Why, then, to the dishonor of my house, hast thou set forth but four? Draw forth from the oldest of my father's vineyards, and bring up of the Falernian that Herod brought me from Rome.' "

Our new acquaintance seemed much pleased, and declared that Nat was right, and that the scene was very like a Roman orgie. It is not often that Nat shows to such good advantage, and I reported his remarks as nearly as I could remember them to Victoria when I came home. " Yes," she replied, "Paul Veronese depicts the senses; to see the soul of man we must look at the paintings of the Florentine School. I have no doubt that Veronese painted up to his highest conceptions; but do you think, Phœbe, that the dear Christ would have assisted at a scene like that? It seems to me the halo about his head would have grown dim with sorrow, or lurid and terrible, at such a carousal."

I told Victoria all about our meeting in the Academy, and then for the first time we realized that after all the Vassar girl had not given us her name.

" From your description, I believe she is Calliope Carter," Victoria remarked, with an air of complete conviction. " I don't think that there is such another absent-minded creature on the whole list of alumni. She was from the West, somewhere. Her father was the captain of the first Mississippi steamboat that carried a calliope, and he was so entranced with its strains that he named his daughter for it. At least, that was the tradition commonly believed at college. Some one started the name Fog-horn, in derision, but she was too gentle and kind to keep a nickname; and although she was very queer, we liked and respected her, and believed in a vague way that her eccentricity was a proof of latent talent. And so she has blossomed into a sculptor! Well, I am not surprised."

5

"But, Victoria, we do not even know to a certainty that she is a Vassar girl at all. That was only Nat's supposition."

Still, Victoria's belief was unshaken, and she decided to go with me when I went to call upon our new acquaintance.

I was completely exhausted after so much sight-seeing; the staring upward, too, tired my neck and made me dizzy, and I was glad enough to get back to my couch. Victoria tucked me up with an air that was both maternal and professional.

"I have been studying up your case while you were gone," she said; "you must have hot milk, raw eggs, and go to bed every night at eight o'clock."

"But Mrs. Richlands has invited us to her reception to-morrow evening, and I want to go so much. You must really let me this time."

"We will see how you are to-morrow. Shut your eyes now, and go to sleep."

I am going to shock Victoria. She thinks I am a great deal more sensible than I am; but one might as well be honest at the start. I am afraid I am a very recreant Vassar girl. All of the alumni that I have met have elevated aims, and are interested in philanthropy or science or art. Now I don't care a pin for any of these things. I adore society; and I mean to be a society woman! That assertion, now that I have written it, looks so very depraved that I am ashamed of it; but it's the truth, nevertheless. I would exult in giving elegant dinners and lawn-parties and fêtes, and having people boast of being invited to one of my very choice receptions. Really, it would be the life of a queen, — for what else are queens good for? I wonder whether Victoria will give me up when she knows to what a low standard I aspire.

CHAPTER V.

A SOCIETY WOMAN.

THE reception at Mrs. Richlands' was delightful. Victoria would have gone, but Uncle Jonah had an attack of sciatica, and she decided to stay at home and read to him, for Aunt Pen had quite set her heart on having this little glimpse at Italian society; and though she hung away her seal-skin sacque when Uncle began to groan, we knew that it must be a heavy disappointment for her. She put on her most elaborate bonnet with great alacrity when Victoria assured her that she would be glad to be allowed to remain at home. And I believe she was really glad, though I cannot understand how one can prefer a lonely evening to a gay party. It turned out, too, that she and Nat had guessed correctly. Our new friend is a Vassar girl, and her name is Calliope Carter. She belongs to a set that graduated several years ago; our class call them Antediluvians. She was delighted to hear of Victoria Delavan, and asked after Maud Van Vechten, Delight Holmes, Barbara Atchison, Cecilia Boylston, and loads of others, of whom I have only a dim idea that they are buried, or married, or famous, or have fulfilled their earthly lot in some other way. I was much more interested in watching the panorama of Mrs. Richlands' guests than in hearing about these ancient worthies. Nearly all the company were strangers in Venice. Two oldish young English ladies, with their father, an East India officer, were introduced to me, and proved to be very frigid and uninteresting. There was an Austrian general all ablaze with stars and crosses, who wore terrific whiskers and was ridiculously proud of his broken English; a young French artist also, who was very melancholy and probably very poor; several Americans besides ourselves; and a German countess who was a sight to behold. Count Torlonia escorted us, and was decidedly the most distinguished-appearing person present. The only other Italian of whose nationality I was sure from his looks was a musician with a waxed mustache, who whisked his coat-skirts just as Gough used to do, and played what I should have called a capriccio, but what Mrs. Richlands announced as a toccata. Count Torlonia asked me if I remembered Robert Browning's "A Toccata of Galuppi's,"

A TOCCATA AT MRS. RICHLANDS'.

and I was ashamed to say that I did not. He quoted from it at length, and since then I have looked it up.

"What they lived once thus at Venice, where the merchants were the kings,
Where St. Mark's is, where the Doges used to wed the sea with rings, —
Ay, because the sea 's the street there ; and 't is arched by — what you call
Shylock's bridge with houses on it, where they kept the carnival."

A VENETIAN GARDEN.

This led to our discussing the " Merchant of Venice," and wondering that there was so little really Venetian in the background of the play. The Count has promised to take us to see the Rialto, and Nat is going down the lagoon to see an argosy.

Mrs. Richlands lives in a beautiful suite of rooms on the Grand Canal, furnished in palatial style with bric-a-brac which she has picked up during a ten years' residence at the different capitals of Europe. At one end of the long apartment there is a fresco copied from a painting by Paul Veronese representing a Venetian garden in the sixteenth century. The perspective was so skilfully managed that you seemed to look away down a long vista of garden walk to a triumphal arch in the background. In the middle distance a servant was setting a table beneath a vine-canopied pavilion upheld by stone caryatides, while in the foreground richly dressed ladies were stepping down the marble stairs into a gondola. I was looking at this picture while the gentleman from Milan played the toccata ; and the ladies in the laced bodices and powdered hair looked so youthful and gay that I could almost hear them saying, " Yes, we lived thus once at Venice."

On a beautiful Renaissance cabinet of ebony, with ivory inlay, Mrs. Richlands had displayed some old Venetian glass, — tall goblets with twisted stems, some of them iridescent and others jewelled or covered with a lace-like filigree, and all looking too fragile to touch, though they were very old. Count Torlonia, seeing me interested, said that he had a Millefiori glass said to have once been the property of Lucrezia Borgia, and from which she habitually drank ; as it was so composed that, if it were filled with a liquid containing the cele-brated Borgia poison, it would instantly fly in pieces.

Take it all in all, I had a charming evening at Mrs. Richlands', but I paid for it this morning with a racking headache. Nat says it was the supper, and if we had put the salad into Lucrezia Borgia's glass it would have shivered into a thousand atoms. I feel better

after my long morning nap. Every one has gone away to see the
Ducal Palace and the Bridge of Sighs. I am rather glad to have es-
caped visiting the prison; but I would have liked to go with them to
the Palace of the Doges at the other end of the bridge, and have seen

VENETIAN GLASS.

the Giants' Staircase, with its statues of Mars and Neptune, and the
portraits of the seventy-six doges in the Library, with the blank place
for the traitor Marino Falieri; but sight-seeing requires the strength
of a Hercules. I think I am quite right in deciding to be nothing
but a society woman, for I have n't the health to accomplish anything
grand.

FOUR O'CLOCK TEA.

I wish Nat were here to read to me. I wanted to finish the " Life of Titian " before leaving Venice ; but my eyes will not let me read. I am a little lonely.

Ah! here comes Victoria with a glass of lemonade. " You dear girl, I thought you had gone. with the rest, or perhaps that you were disgusted with me on account of my superficial views of life."

And then Victoria sat down beside me and talked with me so lovingly and sisterly that my heart was drawn to her more than ever. I want to write down what she said while it is fresh in my mind, that I may have it to refer to by and by. She has formed too high an esti- mate of me; but no matter. I shall be the better for this glimpse into what might be.

" My dear Phœbe," she said, " I am not surprised that you aspire to be a leader in society. In some respects you are well fitted to become one; and when I think of what is in the power of a woman ruling over such an empire, a career of this kind seems to me one of the noblest that can be chosen."

I opened my eyes wide. " Victoria Delavan! Do you mean to say that to give dinner parties and afternoon teas is nobler than to paint pictures or to write stories? "

" It may be, for life itself is higher than the arts of life. The painter or the writer only depicts an ideal existence. The society woman lives her life, if any one can be said to live, and she touches the lives of a thousand different persons. Take one such afternoon tea, for instance, which you will give one of these days, and at which there may be thirty or forty guests. How much tact and experience, diplomatic skill and kindness of heart, has gone to the making up of that little company! There is a shy genius coaxed from his den by your sunny powers of persuasion. He never goes anywhere — he cannot bear society twaddle; but Miss Todd is so charming, and has such a knack of bringing together interesting people, that it is a privilege to attend one of her delightful gatherings; one is refreshed and inspired by exquisite music, intellectual and witty conversation. It is something to have touched the hand of this eminent man, to have studied the face of this noble woman. And the eminent man is rested, amused ; the wealthy woman finds some one to patronize; the unknown musician is introduced; the rising poet is applauded, and helped to wider appreciation ; the dramatic genius is recognized, and finds his foot planted a little more firmly on the ladder of fame ; and the profound thinker, who knows he is not a society man, brings his garnered thought, and the minds of all present are touched by an electric spark, elevating or stimulating; while the student himself, from being a mere bookworm, is won to the study of the great book of human nature. Then, too, in a lull in the sparkling conversation a singer may let fall such a pearl of a song that eyelids will be moistened and hearts touched as though he sang from the choir of a great cathedral. Young girls will confess that an entertainment of this kind is really more interesting than a german, and will envy your remarkable conversational powers. The younger men see that to shine in such society requires an ability to converse on other than the merest commonplaces of the day. Friendless people make congenial acquaintances ; philanthropists have a hearing; the stranger is welcomed; the foreigner carries back to the Old World a higher opinion of America. There is not a person present who has not been helped or who has not aided another. The evening has been a sermon on charity and good-will; and yet no one goes away with the consciousness that he has been preached at. Such a hostess is a queen indeed, and the opportunities which she may improve for doing good are incalculable."

I had listened to all this with a kindling enthusiasm, delighted to find that my ambition was really a worthy one; but suddenly an overwhelming sense of the genius and the labor necessary to the making of such a hostess came over me. " I do not believe there ever was just such a manager," I said. " She would need the mind of a Napoleon to arrange her campaigns, and that other general, whoever he was, who knew the name of every soldier in his army."

" Yes," Victoria admitted, " a special aptitude is required, but the world has known many such women. The salons of Madame de Staël and Madame Récamier were notable instances." And she named other leaders in our own country who have this remarkable faculty.

" And what makes you think I have it?" I asked.

" Nat told me of the club you organized among the young people of your home; how it started out with the idea of acting, — an amateur theatrical company, — but broadened into a lyceum; and of your mission Sunday-school work, and the fair for the day nursery. All these things required management of people, and you seem to have known how to make all work together harmoniously." It seemed, too, that I had betrayed myself in my talks about Vassar; for I was popular with the girls, though not with the teachers, and was always on committees, and a prime mover and head conspirator in the way of frolics. I began to feel quite happy to find that Victoria appreciated me; but I confided to her that my vacations were really more trying for my health than the regular college work.

" I can well believe it," Victoria replied; " there is no career which demands such a strong physique as that of a society woman. Perfect health is one of her absolute requirements, and the most necessary one."

" Then I might as well give up at the outset."

" No. Let your ambition be a spur to your endeavor after it. It is within your power if you try earnestly, but you must not begin your career until you are positive that you have obtained this prime essential. As a minister's wife with a large parish on your hands, or a Mrs. Senator Someone, with all your husband's constituents to look after, you would break down utterly without a good constitution to depend upon; and the creation of a salon requires far more physical labor than one would naturally imagine."

"All right, Victoria, *dottore mia*. Do your best for me, and I promise to do the best I can for myself. I'll abandon society for the present, if you say so, and shut myself up in a health-cure, — anything to become thoroughly well."

Victoria kissed me, and thought we would be able to carry on a little health-cure of our own; and as we heard Nat's voice outside, suggested that we should have a game of battledore and shuttlecock in the corridor. I sprang up from the sofa feeling really quite lively, for her sermon had been an invigorating one, and Nat and I began a hotly contested match. Then we went in to dinner, and I ate so much polenta that Aunt Pen was scandalized.

"Shall I not be able to go out at all in Rome?" I asked Victoria.

"Certainly," she replied; "I hope we shall be able to go out every day."

"But I mean in the evening, — to parties and dinners?"

"Not often; but there are very charming afternoon reunions in Rome which you can attend. I know a Mrs. Clarke, an American who has lived abroad a long time, whom you might well study, for she is an acknowledged leader in Roman society."

"If she will only take us up, I will fathom all the recesses of her soul until I find the secret of her success."

"She is worth your study, and I shall be curious to see whether our estimates agree; and meantime she is sure to make your stay in Rome delightful."

Then the others came noisily in, chatting of all they had seen. Nat, in especial, was jubilant over his visit to the Arsenal, and pouring forth a steady stream of, "You ought to have gone," and, "You don't know what you have lost, — the remains of the old junk 'Bucephalus' — no, I mean 'Bucentaur,' and flags from the battle of Lepanto, and Attila's helmet, and a stone lion from Marathon; and — and — "

Victoria and I could talk no more for that time; but we clasped hands under the afghan, and understood one another perfectly on all points but one. She said something about the necessity of a minister's wife being in some sense a society woman. I don't quite understand her there; and if Victoria thinks that I would under any conditions, no matter how famous he might be, or how much I might care for him, marry a minister — why, Victoria doesn't understand me!

CHAPTER VI.

PADUA. — FERRARA. — BOLOGNA. — PISA.

COUNT TORLONIA has arranged a pilgrimage among the churches for us, which we are to set out upon this afternoon. We will visit the Frari for Titian's sake; and that of the Saints Giovanni and Paolo because the funerals of the doges take place here and their tombs are in the choir; and the Jesuits for its fine marbles; and the Salute to see the great pictures by Titian and Tintoretto in the sacristy; and possibly several more, if enthusiasm and strength hold out.

Victoria had a curious experience this morning. She went out alone, and as she was stepping into her gondola, another approached. She was sure that the gondolier was making for our steps; but the gentleman within leaned out and gave him some direction, whereupon the boat shot quickly off into another canal. The strange part of it is, that as the gentleman leaned out, Victoria recognized him as an American whom she met in Brazil when she was travelling with the Holmeses. She says that he was a very prepossessing man, and that he pretended to be a Brazilian Senhor, but that it was afterwards ascertained that he was a defaulting cashier from the United States. Victoria thinks that he recognized her before she saw him, and this is why he ordered his gondolier to row him in another direction. It is quite exciting. I wonder why he was coming to our palazzo.

Calliope Carter has been here all the morning; she returns to Rome this week, and we are half inclined to go with her.

Nat has been poring over books giving statistics of the commerce of Venice during the Middle Ages, and says he understands how

GIOTTO'S FRESCOS.

Shakspeare intended to represent a capitalist who should correspond to one of our railroad financiers, in Antonio, the Merchant of Venice. The ships were the railroads of Venice. At the close of the fifteenth century she owned three hundred ships, manned by eight thousand sailors, with three thousand smaller craft, not to mention the navy of forty-five galleys with their eleven thousand men. Venice must have been very gay at the time of the Crusades, with her merchants and artists, her knights and nobles, and foreigners from all countries swarming in her canals.

A letter has just arrived from Count Torlonia. He has been called away very suddenly, and will not be able to make the pilgrimage of the churches with us, but he hopes to see us in Rome. With the letter came an old morocco-covered case containing a goblet of antique twisted glass. It is Lucrezia Borgia's cup, which he has given to me. It is much too valuable a present for me to accept, but he has given us no address, and I cannot return it until we see him again. Nat does not believe in its genuineness, and was for trying it with all the poisons at the little chemist's on the next corner; but I have reminded him that it only professes to detect the Borgia recipe.

It is strange, but really a part of Venice seems gone, now that Count Torlonia has left. No one has any enthusiasm to carry out the church-pilgrimage scheme, and we have decided to proceed on our journey with Calliope. We are to wander along slowly, stopping at the interesting places *en route*, and first at

PADUA.

I am writing in the cars; for we only stopped over one train at Padua, lunched at a disagreeable hotel, and were taken by Calliope to see some bronzes by Donatello.

Calliope says that this artist was intensely truth-seeking; that he labored most of all to give an appearance of life to his work.

He would often talk to his statues while modelling, and stepping back, cry impetuously, " Speak, speak ! " I shall look for Donatello again when we reach Florence. Michael Angelo said of his " Saint Mark," in that city, that " one could not fail to believe the gospel preached by such an honest-looking man." We saw some very sweet and childlike angels of his in the Santo, standing on tiptoe and piping their very hearts into their bursting cheeks. I wish I might have them reproduced in small on a music cabinet.

There was one of Giotto's frescos in one of the churches, which I must not forget to mention, chiefly because Nat quite upset the dignity of our entire company by insisting that the angels were mosquitoes.

We are approaching Ferrara, where we will spend the night and as much of to-morrow as we shall be tempted to give it.

FERRARA.

This queer old city has proved so interesting that we have lingered here three days.

In the first place, there is a palace where Lucrezia Borgia gave her poison feast to the young gentlemen of Venice who had once offended her by having her thrust from a ball-room. Then there is the Cathedral, and Tasso's prison, and the Library with the precious manuscripts, — Ariosto's " Orlando Furioso" and Tasso's " Jerusalem Delivered." We have stopped at the Golden Star Hotel, which is not far from these places of interest.

Best of all, the Castle d'Este is here. Its square towers have a charm for me of which I am sure one could never tire, and the lapping water in the moat tells of bloody feuds and crimes. It is one of the most picturesque castles I have ever seen; and when one considers the life histories that have been acted here, I know of none more interesting. The panther woman Lucrezia paced through these halls, which needed, indeed, after that contamination, to be cleansed by the

CASTLE OF FERRARA

presence of some good woman like that of Renate, or Renée, a princess of France and wife of Hercules d'Este. She was a Protestant, and secretly harbored Calvin in one of the towers of this very castle. The castle chapel is still shown where he preached to a few invited guests under the very nose of Pope Julius II.; for Ferrara is one of the papal cities. Mr. Howells quotes from an Italian guide-book which speaks of Renée as follows : —

"This lady was learned in belles lettres and in the schismatic doctrines with which Calvin and Luther agitated the people. Calvin himself, under the name of Huppeville, visited her in Ferrara in 1536, and ended by corrupting her mind and seducing her into his own errors, which produced discord between her and her religious husband, and resulted in his placing her in temporary seclusion in order to attempt her conversion."

The castle extended such free hospitality and entertained, through its different owners, so many celebrated guests, that it was said, —

"Whoe'er in Italy is known to fame,
This lordly house as frequent guest can claim."

One other lady of the family of d'Este, Leonora, the patroness of Tasso, lives still in history. We have all seen pictures of the poet reading to her and to her maids of honor, who, I think, must have yawned at times, — politely, of course, and behind their fans, — unless the readings were very short indeed, and interspersed with much mandolin playing and dancing. I shall try, when I am a social leader, to find more interesting poets to give readings at my evenings.

One thing which pleased us all very much I must not forget to mention. At the foot of one of the old feudal towers we found a white marble tablet in honor of Garibaldi.

BOLOGNA.

We have just left Bologna, having given it but a few hours, when it deserved as many days. Modena, too, lay off to the right. I would have liked to visit it for the sake of Ginevra, who, it is asserted, never lived there or anywhere else, except in the poet's imagination; and yet she is so much a real personage to us, that we never see one of the long carved chests so common in Italy, without wondering whether it might not have been the one which coffined her young life in.

The most interesting things to me in Bologna were two statues, kneeling angels, which serve as candelabra, one of which was sculptured by Michael Angelo before he was widely famous. Italy is full of beautiful statues. I made that rather trite remark the other day, and Nat replied, —

"Yes; it makes me think of 'Wilhelm Meister:' —

'Die Marmorbilder steht und seht mir an.'

You know the poem, of course?"

"No," I replied; "I have not studied German."

"Well, then, I must translate it for you: —

'The marble statues stand and stare;
They freeze my blood, they lift my hair;
They clasp their hands, and beg and weep,
Come buy your tombstone, we're *so* cheap!'"

Nat is such a rascal! Without joking, however, I do intend to buy a kind of tombstone. I asked Uncle Jonah if he would be willing to have one made for me in Italy when I died, and he said, "Certainly, dear child!"—"And how high would you be willing to pay?" He supposed that the correct thing would cost a thousand or fifteen hundred dollars. "Then," said I, "please order it now." Uncle Jonah looked anxious. "You don't feel worse, do you, Phœbe?" he asked kindly.

Nat burst into a hearty laugh. "She's getting better every day; but she has struck an economical vein, like the old gentleman in New

CALVIN.

England, who bought a coffin cheap at auction, and kept it under his bed, using the box down cellar as a potato-bin. Phœbe thinks she will never have another chance to buy monuments to such advantage, and of course it will keep. But where do you mean to set it? Have something in the ornamental line, and it will serve as a fountain in the front yard."

"Nat," I said, "I am in earnest. I do not think I am going to die at present. I am going to do all I can to get well; and as I think that is a very joyful event, I want to celebrate it by erecting a statue to Health. When I die, I don't want any monument at all."

Uncle Jonah considered a moment. "I believe you are right," he said. "Only prove to me that you are soundly well, and that I shall not have to be asked to contribute right away to another monument, and you may have your tombstone now."

I gave Uncle Jonah a frantic hug, and turning to Calliope, exclaimed, "Do you hear that? You have my commission to model a statue of Health, for fifteen hundred dollars, if that is enough."

Calliope smiled. "That is a very good price," she said. "But how do you know that I can do anything; and where is the statue to be placed?"

"I know you can, to the first question; and to the second — I want it placed in the new gymnasium which they are going to build at Vassar."

"Not too fast," Victoria suggested; "you have not yet fulfilled your uncle's conditions."

"I only accept conditionally," Calliope replied. "I will model my idea of Hygeia in clay, and you shall then feel perfectly free to order it or not, as you choose."

So we have left the matter; but I know I shall be satisfied. I like Calliope, but she is queer as queer can be. In the first place, she avoids people, especially rich and fashionable persons, whom, one would think, it would be to her interest to cultivate. She has an

absurd idea that a girl with a career has no time to waste on society;
and I know that she looks down upon me, not in a scornful but in a
pitying way, as a girl of low ambitions. I unintentionally overheard a
scrap of conversation between her and Victoria. Calliope's remark
ended with, " a pity she has
not a higher ideal." And Victoria replied, " We do not long
for the best at first; and Phœbe
will be either led on from this
low ambition to a higher, or she
will ennoble the end itself by en-
dowing it with such new dignity
that it will be worth striving for."

Nat was not pleased with our
visit at Bologna. He ordered
sausage for lunch, and he says
it was *not* genuine Bologna.
He cannot believe that he has
been deceived all his life, and
that what he has known as Bologna sausage is a fraud; and
therefore he insists that the city
we have just left is not Bologna, but some unprincipled hamlet
masquerading under that celebrated name.

A RAVENNESE.

Some Italians from Ravenna had the same compartment with
us, and had brought an enormous lunch-basket from which they
constantly refreshed themselves with fried cakes and bananas.

Nat says he is glad to have met these Ravennese, for now he
understands the derivation of the word ravenous. The sight of so
much food made me almost ill, and we changed our compartment.
We have now as travelling companions a far more agreeable Florentine family, with a sweet little girl restless as a sprite, with whom Nat

is scraping acquaintance by making a puppet-show with knots tied in his handkerchief.

We have had a shocking accident. The train was stopping at some village, and little Beatrice was looking out with her hand upon

THE ACCIDENT.

the door, when the guard came along and banged it to, shutting three of the child's fingers into the crevice. I think we all shrieked, with the exception of the little girl; she turned perfectly white, but was so still you might have thought the shock had killed her. It seemed an age before we could get that door opened, and then the child fainted. They stopped the train; but we were miles from any town, and the father cried in agony, " Is there no physician on board?" "I am almost one," Victoria replied modestly, and immediately set about doing just the right thing. The fingers were lacerated as well as crushed, and some of the bones were broken. I buried my face in my wraps, but Nat acted as hospital steward, helping Victoria, and shredding the knotted handkerchief for bandages.

Victoria said that the only aid which she could then render was temporary, as there must be an operation when they reached home, which was fortunately quite near. The family were overwhelmingly grateful, and begged her so earnestly to go with them and continue the care of the child until they could secure the services of their own physician, that I gave up my own claim upon her and joined my entreaties to theirs. We had not intended to stop at Florence on our way to Rome, for we are in haste to reach the winter-quarters already engaged for us, and are reserving the beautiful city on the Arno until warm weather shall drive us from Rome. Uncle Jonah did not see fit to change his plans even now. "Miss Delavan can join us as soon as the little girl no longer requires her attention," he said. And so, disguising as much as possible our dislike at parting from her, though only for a few days, we left her, like the good Samaritan she is, with these new friends who needed her so much, and hastened on to

PISA.

We have just left the city of the Leaning Tower, and are speeding along the coast toward Civita Vecchia and Rome. We were only in Pisa long enough to see the Cathedral, the Baptistery, and the Campanile. I have always thought that the inclination of the Tower must be exaggerated, and was almost startled when I saw it apparently toppling to its fall. Aunt and I could not be persuaded to ascend it; but Uncle and Nat mounted its eight stories, and brought back accounts of a wide-stretching view, — Leghorn plainly visible, and Corsica a blue line in the distance. There is a chime of bells in the top, of sweet, full tone. The largest bell is named Pasquareccia. It is only tolled when criminals are led out to execution. The Tower is over seven hundred years old, and no one knows when it began to settle. The most beautiful thing in the Cathedral, to my thinking, was a pulpit resting on seven pillars, each alternate one having for its base a crouching lion.

In the Baptistery we saw the swinging bronze lamp which first suggested to Galileo, then only eighteen years old, the use of the pendulum as an exact measurer of time. Some of his experiments with falling bodies were performed from the top of the Leaning Tower. What stupendous facts were developed later by this great astronomer, all hingeing on the simple swinging of this censer lamp! He was summoned before the Inquisition to answer for his heretical assertion of the motion of the earth, and was weak enough to

LEANING TOWER.

recant it; though tradition states that he followed the abjuration with the whisper, *E pur si muove*, — "Nevertheless, it does move."

One realizes these historic words even in snail-paced Italy. The Inquisition has passed away, and Galileo's heresy is triumphant even here. Father Secchi, the astronomer monk, in his convent observatory, used Galileo's inventions and theories. Everywhere, in science, politics, religion, "the old order changes, giving place to new." The world does move.

CHAPTER VII.

OLD ROME.

General View. — The Forum and the Capitol.

"Over the dumb Campagna sea,
  Out in the offing, through mist and rain,
  Saint Peter's church heaves silently,
  Like a mighty ship in pain."

As we approached Rome and could see, through gaps in the ruined aqueduct almost before the city itself was visible, the dome of St. Peter's rising on the horizon, these lines came to my mind. All Italy, to me, is stamped with the thought of the Brownings. How wonderful it must be to think or say anything which through all time will

THE CAMPAGNA.

be connected with a certain place, and such a place as Rome, where so many minds have thought and eloquent tongues have spoken, that it would seem there was not an idea left to be voiced.

We have taken rooms in a queer flatiron-shaped building, with our parlor in the point, and a window which looks down two streets. I have not been out yet; but Nat has already found the principal streets

THE AVENTINE.

and squares. I turn to the map[1] and he gives me a general survey of
the city. It is divided by the Tiber into two unequal parts. That
on the left is Rome proper; Trastevere is on
the right. The business quarter of the city
is situated in the lower part, on the site of
the old Campus Martius. The principal
street here is the Corso, one mile in length,
from the Piazza del Popolo to the foot of
the Capitol Hill, and is lined with handsome
palaces. The Piazza del Popolo is a public
square with an Egyptian obelisk in the centre, and from it extend diagonally the Via
Ripetta and the Via del Babuino, which opens
into the Piazza di Spagna, — the strangers'
quarter, — near which we have taken lodgings.
Nat wandered down to the river-bank at
the foot of the Capitol and the Palatine, and
found the Ghetto, or Jews' quarter, and on
through its labyrinthine alleys to the Aventine, Palatine, and Cælian Hills, covered with
vineyards, convents, and ruins. He says the
Pincian and Quirinal Hills are the abode of
the upper class in more senses than one, for
the inhabitants of the palaces and villas that
crown their summits breathe purer air and
enjoy a more widely extended view, and their
grounds are terraced and laid out in grand
old gardens. Between these two hills he
found the Barberini Palace, and on the

THE AMERICAN IN ROME.

Quirinal is the Pontifical Palace, fronting the Square of Castor and
Pollux. On the left bank are St. Peter's, the Vatican, and the Castle

---

[1] See map of Rome, inside cover.

of St. Angelo.   Nat has amused us by an account of the people whom he has seen in his wanderings.   He was not so much interested in the natives as in other sight-seers, whom he calls "strangers in Rome, Jews and proselytes."   He described one American whose peculiar cast of countenance and shaven upper lip seemed to proclaim him a Massachusetts farmer, but who wore a sombrero that would have become a Texas ranch-man, who gazed at the statues and shook his head, muttering, "Shades of Anthony Comstock!"   He saw the old English officer from India, whom we met in Venice, wandering about, snarling and grumbling at everything, while his startled daughter looked as if she would have been glad to admire but dared not.

I am disappointed in Uncle Jonah; he has an idea that women are not thorough, and says that he hates to have business dealings with them, for they always enlist his sympathies, and sympathy will bankrupt any business.

THE ENGLISH OFFICER AND HIS DAUGHTER.

Uncle Jonah is vestryman of the Church of St. ——, at home, and he had a rather disagreeable experience with the soprano, who was the real leader of the choir, and selected all the music to suit her own voice.   "Really," he said to Aunt Pen, "I can't get along with her at all; we must have a man in that position."   Even Aunt Pen could not help laughing at that; and she has not ceased asking Uncle Jonah if he has yet found his gentleman soprano.

It is too bad that I have failed in showing him that a girl can teach Latin.   Nat sees my grief, and is truly repentant.   He told Uncle

ROMAN FORUM.

that it was all his fault; I was a good teacher, but he was a poor learner.

"Oh, yes!" sniffed Uncle Jonah; "any one can keep school if the pesky children are kept away. I want to find some one who will teach you in spite of yourself."

He called at Calliope's studio this morning, and says he is on the track of some one, — a young theological student just back from a tour through the Holy Land, who is staying awhile in Rome. Calliope thinks he will be willing to take Nat in charge for a time. His name is Hathaway. Nat says he will not have his way with him, and confides to me his resolution not to learn a particle, to show his father that it wasn't my fault. This is very consoling to me; but I must counsel Nat to be a good boy, though I know I shall be jealous of the new tutor's success.

He has come. I knew I should not like him, so his commonplace appearance is no disappointment. But I am weary of the view from the window, and to-morrow we are to accept his guidance through the ruins, beginning with old Rome, coming down, in the course of centuries, if we live long enough, to more interesting modern art.

Evening. We have made a beginning, and have just returned from a visit to the Roman Forum, where so many noted ruins cluster, and from the Capitol, where the photograph was taken which I now insert. On the left are eight Ionic columns belonging to the Temple of Saturn; between these we can see indistinctly the white Phocian Column. In the distance is the great pile of the Coliseum, just in front of which rises the campanile of Santa Francesca. To the extreme right are three Corinthian columns, — all that is left of the Temple of Castor and Pollux. Mr. Hathaway talked in a really interesting strain of these old temples, and we loitered along a pleasant road, shaded by trees, to where the Arch of Titus gave us another vista. Here his enthusiasm quite overflowed in his attempt to make us realize what this part of Rome must have been when this arch was erected. He has returned fresh from a study of Jerusalem and the Temple, sacked by the Roman legions, and it is all as real to him as though it occurred yesterday. I could not share his enthusiasm, but I could see that it was not the least bit affected. As we stood there he read from Mrs. Hawthorne: —

" Through this [arch] I perceive, coming on, the triumph of Titus, after his conquest of Jerusalem, and behold, glittering in the sun, the sacred seven-branched candlestick of massive gold, borne by the procession, and the silver trumpets of Judah, and the golden table from the Temple of temples, the Temple of Jerusalem. And here is the Emperor in his car, with four proudly stepping horses, surrounded by the bearers of the fasces, and crowned by Victory.'

The Forum is a valley between the Capitol and the Palatine. We passed the Arch of Septimius Severus as we descended from the Capitol. It is quite modern for this part of Rome, for it was erected A. D. 203, to commemorate victories over the Arabians and Parthians, who are represented on its bas-reliefs.

To-night we visit the Coliseum, and this afternoon I shall read all I can, in preparation, from the "Students' Gibbon" and other histories. I have also been looking over photographs of pictures by Piloty, Alma Tadema, Kaulbach, Wagner, and others.

I know now the position of the Seven Hills, — the Pincian, Quirinal, Viminal, Esquiline, Palatine, Cælian, and Aventine. They follow very nearly the curve of the Tiber, and across its tawny water we see the Vatican Hill and Janiculum, which we all remembered from Macaulay's grand poem, " Horatius," —

> "For since Janiculum is lost,
> What hope to save the town?"

Nat had occasion to quote from it more than once; it is as true to the topography as a guide-book, and yet thrilling all through with vivid human interest. The Museum of the Capitol stands where the citadel was situated which the Gauls attempted to surprise one night

GEESE OF THE CAPITOL.

away back in the early history of Rome, nearly five hundred years before the Christian era; but the geese gave the alarm and saved the city. Nat was greatly interested in that incident; he said he should never say, "as silly as a goose," again. We saw a consequential old gander stalking about the hill, and Nat very politely gave him a military salute; for he said that it was possible that his two thousand times great grandfather might have been one of the faithful sentries. The principal buildings on the Capitol now are three palaces forming the three sides of a square, in the centre of which is a fine bronze statue of Marcus Aurelius. It was formerly gilt, and some traces of gold are still to be seen upon it.

One of these buildings, the Capitoline Museum, we entered, to study its fine collection of the statuary of antiquity; and whom should we find here but Count Torlonia? I thought at first that he was not really glad to see us. He kept looking about in a furtive way as though he expected some one else to join us, but we were all there. Nat noticed his manner, and said, "You are looking for Miss Delavan? We left her in Florence."

It seemed to me that he looked relieved; but he only said, "I have not had the pleasure of meeting Miss Delavan. Is she a relative of yours?"

Now I think of it, he did not happen to see her when we were in Venice, and I suppose I must have imagined his queer behavior, for I cannot think of any reason for it. At all events, he was pleasant enough afterward, and chatted about the statues in a very entertaining way. He invited us to make an excursion to his villa somewhere on the way to Naples, where he says he has made some astonishing discoveries, and is having excavations carried on in behalf of the " Société pour le Vol des Monumens Anciens." Uncle Jonah was very much interested in his account of a Hygeia which had been recently unearthed.

" It would be just the thing. Phœbe," he said, " for the Vassar Gymnasium."

" But, Uncle," I protested, " I have ordered a statue from Calliope; it would not be fair to her to change."

" You did not exactly order it, you know," Aunt Pen urged, " and I should think a real antique would be much more classical, and suitable to a college."

" If it is a real antique," Nat suggested, " it will be sure not to have any nose or arms."

" The statues here are many of them very ancient," the Count replied, " and most of them are in a good state of preservation ; " and

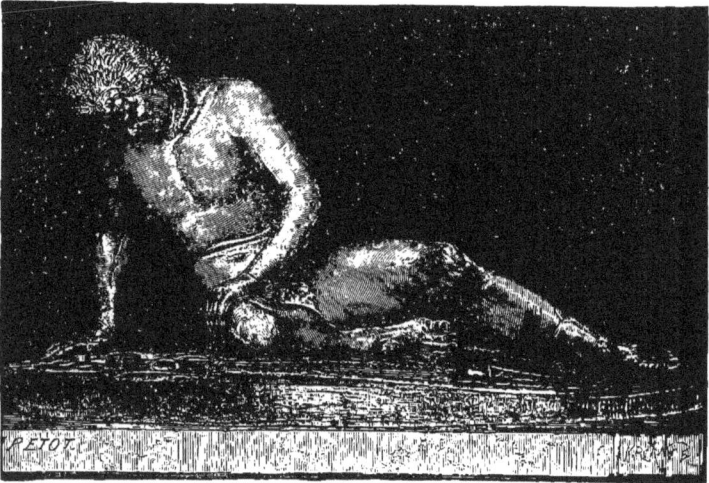

WOUNDED GAUL.

then the conversation passed to the wonderful marbles and bronzes by which we were surrounded. We paid our respects first to the " Marble Faun," which Hawthorne has made familiar to Americans, with his smiling face and pointed ears ; and here too we found the " Dying Gladiator," which Mr. Hathaway says is falsely so called, and is really a

SQUARE OF THE CAPITOL.

dying Gaul. He steadies himself with one hand on the ground, but his strength is lapsing with his life-blood, and he sinks heavily downward. Mr. Hathaway pointed out the collar which proclaims the man a Gaul of Julius Cæsar's time, and then spoke so entertainingly of Cæsar's campaigns that Nat was stirred with emulation to re-read the unappreciated Gallic Wars. It was in the old Capitol that Cæsar was murdered, and we saw the famous statue of Pompey, at whose feet the great ruler expired. In this building we found also the Venus of the Capitol, and the Antinous, the most perfect representation of youthful manhood which has come down to us from antiquity. We were especially interested in the collection of portrait busts of the real men of ancient Rome who walked once in the Forum below. Here are the long line of Cæsars, of whom Story writes in his "Roba di Roma:" "At Rome the Emperors become as familiar as the Popes. Who does not know the curly-headed Marcus Aurelius? Are there any modern portraits more familiar than the severe wedge-like head of Augustus,

AUGUSTUS.

or the dull phiz of Hadrian, with his hair combed down over his low forehead, or the vain perking face of Lucius Verus, or the brutal bull-head of Caracalla, or the bestial, bloated features of Vitellius?"

Here, too, are many of the proud Roman ladies, — Livia, Antonia, Drusilla, Poppæa, Octavia, Statilia, Julia, Faustina, Portia, and a host of others, some as noble as beautiful, and others profligate and shameless. Nat electrified us all by his discovery that these busts were

AGRIPPINA.

adorned with movable marble wigs; and Mr. Hathaway explained that the empresses had their busts sculptured in this way so that when the prevailing fashion in hair-dressing changed, another style could be substituted.

A seated statue of Agrippina, wife of Germanicus and mother of

Caligula, particularly struck me, — a noble woman, whom we must admire for her virtues and pity for her misfortunes. We found Virgil
calmly sweet, a realization of the poet and lover of Nature.

VIRGIL.

Uncle Jonah seemed plunged in profound meditation; he turned to
Mr. Hathaway and asked, "The sculptors of antiquity were usually
men, were they not?"

Mr. Hathaway replied that he had never heard of a woman among
the ancient sculptors, but that Harriet Hosmer held a prominent

8

place among the modern ones. Uncle Jonah was not satisfied. "I have never liked the plan of your having your statue carved by a woman, Phœbe," he grumbled; "it is sure not to be satisfactory."

And so it was agreed that before the winter is over we are to run down to the Count's villa and take a look at the excavations. I shall put it off until Victoria comes, for otherwise I fear that they will all be too much for me, and I am determined not to disappoint Calliope.

Count Torlonia wished to make an appointment for to-morrow, to take us to St. Peter's and to make a pilgrimage of churches in Rome, such as we planned in Venice but did not carry out. Uncle Jonah told him that we were taking things systematically, and had not yet finished ancient Rome; that Mr. Hathaway had planned a programme for to-morrow, to include souvenirs of the early Christians. The Count rather turned up his nose at this, and spoke in a slighting way of Mr. Hathaway, saying that it was not well to place one's self too completely in the hands of a guide. I explained that Mr. Hathaway was not a guide, but Nat's tutor, and a clergyman; but evidently what I said made little impression, for when the Count next spoke to him he addressed him as "Hathaway," as though he were a servant. I don't care in the least for Mr. Hathaway, and I did rather like the Count; but this rudeness fired my indignation, and I stood up for the little minister and would not hear to his plans being set aside. So to-morrow we are going to the Catacombs; and as the Count could not prevail upon us to accompany him, he has asked leave, which we could not well refuse, to go with us.

After leaving the Capitol we stood for a few moments on the edge of the Tarpeian Rock, over which traitors were thrown. The old times were full of crime and cruelty, and I am glad that the tricolor floats over the Rome of to-day and the fasces are buried in oblivion.

CHAPTER VIII.

THE EARLY CHRISTIANS.

THE COLISEUM. — MAMERTINE PRISON AND THE CATACOMBS.

WE visited the great amphitheatre last night by moonlight. It was like a picture. The cavernous arches made black masses of shadow, and the moonshine lay white in the broad arena. It is certainly the most imposing ruin left of ancient Rome. Begun by Vespasian, it was finished by captive Jews under Titus. While we were walking yesterday in the Forum, I noticed that a pretty dark-eyed boy made quite a détour to go around the Arch of Titus. Mr. Hathaway explained that he was a Jew, and his people even to-day cannot be induced to pass under this monument to the downfall of their city and temple.

We walked about the long tiers of seats which once afforded room for nearly ninety thousand spectators, and tried to imagine how it must have looked crowded with the Roman populace; the élite as well as the lower classes thronging the entrances of the "greatest show on earth," singing such songs as Bulwer has imagined : —

> " Ho ! ho ! for the merry, merry show,
>   With a forest of faces in every row !
>   Lo ! the swordsmen bold as the son of Alcmena
>   Sweep side by side o'er the hushed arena.
>   Talk while you may ; you will hold your breath
>   When they meet in the grasp of the glowing death.
>   Tramp, tramp, how gayly they go !
>   Ho ! ho ! for the merry, merry show ! "

I could imagine the combatants lifting their hands to the Emperor before the contest, and crying, " O Cæsar, we who are about to die salute thee." I could imagine the prisoners from Gaul and Africa, the barbaric music, the clash of arms, and the roar of the lions. But the terrible play of the gladiators, and the wild chariot races, sink into insignificance beside the innumerable company of martyrs who were here given to the beasts.

Mr. Hathaway repeated Professor Boyesen's graphic description of Calpurnia's search for the dead bodies of her parents after the cruel " sports," on such a night as this. The painting of the background was so true to nature that I could almost fancy the stealthy footsteps of the lions : —

> " Hushed and empty beneath, as if touched with a chilly remoteness,
> Lay the white square of the Forum, where loomed the Phocian Column
> High in the moon-bathed stillness. · The sculptured arch of Severus
> Glimmered palely amidst the temples of deified Cæsars ;
> While 'neath the brow of the Palatine Hill the vast Coliseum
> Flung its mantle of gloom, to hide the deeds of the darkness
> Wrought on this terrible day for the joy of a barbarous people.
> Sheltered deep in the shade of those huge and cavernous portals
> Stood, close pressed to the stone, a little quivering maiden.
> Fearless she stood, and with burning eyes through the iron-barred gateway
> Gazed at the sated beasts that yawning drowsed in the shadow, —
> Drowsed, or slunk with velveted tread o'er the starlit arena ;
> Snuffing, perchance, as they went, the mangled form of a martyr,
> Sightless, that stared with insensible orbs to the moon-flooded heavens."

The arena was very quiet and peaceful, only one other human being besides our own party within its enclosure, and he a cadaverous pilgrim, pacing slowly from station to station (as the little booth-like chapels which the Roman Church has set up within the enclosure are called) with an open breviary before him, his thin lips moving as in prayer, though I doubt if he could see the words. But in spite of the peaceful stillness it all came upon me with terrible vividness, — the cost of being a Christian in those times ; the nobility of standing by one's conviction even unto death.

TOMB OF CECILIA METELLA.

This morning we drove in an open barouche along the Appian Way to the catacombs of St. Calixtus. The view was superb and the air delicious, the Count was gay and sparkling; but the Coliseum still cast its shadow over my spirits, and his wit seemed to me out of place and flippant. I could not help thinking how many mangled forms had been brought from the Coliseum by night over this very road, to be buried in the underground cells of the Catacombs.

We drove on as far as the great round tomb of Cecilia Metella, its fine marbles stripped away by the Popes to adorn their palaces. Byron's description of this tomb, though it lacks to me the interest of the other poems which I have quoted, yet makes the most of the material, and deserves that a. part of it at least should find a place in my journal : —

A PILGRIM.

> " There is a stern round tower of other days,
> Firm as a fortress, with its fence of stone.
>
>   .   .   .   .
>
> What was this tower of strength? within its cave
> What treasure lay so locked, so hid? — A woman's grave.
> But who was she, the lady of the dead,
> Tombed in a palace?
>
>   .   .   .   .
>
> Perchance she died in youth ; it may be, bowed
> With woes far heavier than the ponderous tomb
> That weighed upon her gentle dust.
>
>   .   .   .   .

> Perchance she died in age, surviving all, —
> Charms, kindred, children, with the silver gray
> On her long tresses, which might yet recall,
> It may be, still a something of the day
> When they were braided, and her proud array
> And lovely form were envied, praised, and eyed
> By Rome. — But whither would conjecture stray?
> Thus much we know, — Metella died,
> The wealthiest Roman's wife. Behold his love or pride ! "

After inspecting the great tomb we turned again toward Rome, and the carriage paused beside a gateway. We descended a steep flight of steps, and found ourselves in the first story of the cemetery of St. Calixtus, for these subterranean labyrinths descend continually, and double upon themselves. There are sometimes three or four strata of the long galleries, lined on each side with tombs cut in the rock like berths in a steamer. The passages were generally narrow, so that we walked in single file, following a snuffy old man with a torch, whom Nat called the Janitor, as though the place were an apartment house. We saw the small earthenware lamps which the Christians used. We entered first the Crypt of Lucina. This Lucina is supposed to be the Christian name of Pomponia Græcina, the wife of Plautus, a noble Roman lady of whom

THE JANITOR OF THE CATACOMBS.

THE ARENA OF THE COLISEUM.

Tacitus wrote: "She was accused of having embraced the rites of a foreign superstition, and though after investigation pronounced innocent, she lived to a great age in continued sadness."

Next we visited the Papal Crypt, where all the early bishops of the Church were buried, and traced the *graffiti*, or scribblings on the wall, of which Northcote makes mention in his " Roma Sotteranea."

These notes by the wayside were made by visitors at the beginning of the Christian era. Some were only names; but one individual had come in search of the tomb of a certain Sofronia, and at the very entrance he had written: *Sofronia, vivas cum tuis,* — " Sofronia, mayest thou live with thine own."

All along the passages this was repeated, a prayer for the soul of the departed; but as he walked, the faith of the pilgrim grew stronger, and on the very tomb he scratched the triumphant realization: *Sofronia dulcis, semper vives Deo,* — " Dear Sofronia, thou wilt ever live in God."

This joyful confidence of the Christians has been contrasted with the gloom of pagan epitaphs. One, to a boy, is mentioned by Northcote, which states that " neither wit nor amiability, nor loving, winning ways had been of avail, but he had become the foul prey of the brutal Pluto."

The pagan epitaphs could only compliment the departed by enumerating his graces and accomplishments; while the earlier Christian inscriptions are characterized by a stern simplicity, and only later appeared such endearing adjectives as "dulcissimus, innocens, and felix." One little boy is spoken of as *agnellus Dei,* — " the little lamb of God." The word " martyr," inscribed after the name, was considered a crown of glory beyond all eulogy. The tombs, or cells, were hollowed in tiers, one above another, usually three or four and sometimes as many as eight, between the floor and ceiling. At intervals the passages widened into chapels and rooms. It was here that the hunted Christians met for worship; these chambers were often decorated with attempts at carving and rude frescos. In the Catacomb of St. Agnes there are pictures from Bible stories, — Jonah sleeping beneath his bower of gourds, and other scenes from the Old Testament; but the favorite design, often repeated, was that of Christ as a shepherd. Mr. Hathaway quoted from a poem about the goats and sheep, — how the early Church wished to show Christ's love for all alike: —

> " And in the Catacombs,
> On those walls subterranean, where she hid
> Her head mid ignominy, death, and tombs,
> She her Good Shepherd's hasty image drew,
> And on his shoulders, not a lamb, a kid."

We noticed the firm belief in the resurrection implied by the inscriptions: the bodies are "deposited," not buried. Sometimes a coin was pressed into the mortar which sealed the tomb, as a means of recognition, and occasionally this was the only marking of the spot. There were places where the coin had dropped away or had been stolen, leaving its impression in the mortar.

I happened to mention that such a coin would have for me all the sacredness of a relic; when the Count remarked that he hoped some day to show us his collection of ancient coins and engraved gems. He wore one silver coin set as a ring, representing what he said he had always considered a Hercules strangling a lion, but if I chose to fancy it a Christian contending in the arena I might do so, and he would be honored by its acceptance. I declined, I fear rather abruptly, and then tried to explain that a ring seemed to me a tiny manacle only to be worn in token of a sacred pledge. We were alone just then, and the Count asked quite seriously, " Then when you wear a ring you will consider yourself bound to the giver? "

HERCULES AND LION.

" Certainly," I replied with decision ; and turning an angle we found ourselves with the others in the Crypt of St. Cecilia. It seemed to me that the Count looked confident and half amused, as though we had laid a wager and he was sure of winning; but I shall not forget this, and cannot imagine myself accepting or wearing a ring presented by

THE PYRAMID OF CESTIUS.

him. I told him that I wished he would allow me to return the Borgia glass; that it made me unhappy to have anything so uncanny in my possession. But he argued very adroitly, that instead of being allied with deeds of evil, its mission was to detect them, and made so light of the gift that it seemed absurd in me to urge him to take it. I wonder why it is that I do not quite like the man, he is so pleasant and plausible. Uncle Jonah trusts him, and he won Aunt Pen's heart by carrying her pug all through the Catacombs. She was so frightened lest it should be lost, and he humored her so courteously and kindly. He is very different from Mr. Hathaway, who is as blunt and honest as can be; but when I imagine both men back in the early days at the Coliseum, some way it seems to me that the Count's place would be beside some lady of fashion, close to the emperor's box, and his tomb at last some costly monument like the pyramid of Cestius, which we saw the other day when visiting the Protestant burying-ground where Keats and Shelley are buried. And Mr. Hathaway,— ah! he would be standing in the centre of the arena with folded arms, waiting the lions.

Of all the poets, I think Robert Browning has expressed best the spirit of the Catacombs in one of its epitaphs which he has thrown into his grand verse : —

> "I was born sickly, poor, and mean,
> A slave ; no misery could screen
> The holders of the pearl of price
> From Cæsar's envy ; therefore twice
> I fought with beasts, and three times saw
> My children suffer by his law.
> At last my own release was earned ;
> I was some time in being burned.
> But at the close a Hand came through
> The fire above my head, and drew
> My soul to Christ, whom now I see.
> Sergius, a brother, writes for me
> This testimony on the wall.
> For me, I have forgot it all."

We drove back to Rome, still on the Appian Way, past the little church of Domine quo Vadis. The legend is a pretty one,— how Peter, fleeing from Rome to escape the persecution of Nero, met the Lord Jesus at this spot, and asked in awe-struck surprise, " Lord, whither goest thou ? " " To Rome," replied the vision, " to suffer again, since my followers flee from martyrdom." Of course tradition states that,

stung by the rebuke, Peter turned about and joyfully confessed Christ
by his death. The authorities say that there is no proof that Peter
was ever in Rome; but the Catholic Church believes it, and Paul
was here, at all events. We visited this afternoon the Mamertine

APPIAN WAY.

Prison, where, it is said, they were both confined, and where hundreds
of other Christians awaited their death-sentence. It is a terrible dun-
geon, in two stories. Prisoners were let down into it by ropes. In
the lower cell they were strangled; and we saw here a walled-up door-
way communicating with a secret way by which the executioners came.

9

In the upper cell is an altar, with roughly carved busts of Peter and Paul. I never saw a more gloomy prison; and yet it was possibly here that Paul wrote the Second Epistle to Timothy, — that loving farewell to his dear friend. I have read it through to-night, every line illu-

THE MAMERTINE PRISON.

mined with new light. Did the jailer allow him a torch and writing material, or was it dictated to the faithful Luke, and by him written from memory? How his great heart yearned for his friend, — " Do thy diligence to come shortly unto me "! And how glorious is the declaration which he makes in the face of death: " For I am now ready to be offered, and the time of my departure is at hand. I have fought

THE MADONNA.

a good fight, I have finished my course, I have kept the faith: henceforth there is laid up for me a crown of righteousness, which the Lord, the righteous Judge, shall give me at that day; and not to me only, but unto all them also that love his appearing."

Could a society woman say that?

I begin to realize what Victoria meant when she said, "Either she will be led on from a low ambition to a higher, or she will ennoble the end itself."

I am sure that God made me for society. I love it, and people say I am a born leader. If that is true, there comes in a responsibility which I have never faced, — I must lead right. Some people are called to work in the slums, among the outcasts, the ignorant, and the poor. I wonder if my field may not be to work for Christ among the idle daughters, — girls who have education and position, and find time hanging heavy on their hands? My brain is buzzing with new ideas. I must leave thinking at once and sleep; but when Victoria comes, I will talk it over with her.

CHAPTER IX.

A LETTER FROM FLORENCE.

NAT has just brought me a letter from Victoria: —

CASA BELLA, November 18.

DEAR LITTLE PHŒBE, — I know you are anxious to hear from me and from my small patient. And Beatrice really deserves that name, for a more gentle and patient little creature I never met. I will not tell you all the details, how several operations have been necessary to remove the splintered bones ; suffice it that she is a little heroine, and that she is so far on the road to recovery that I shall join you ere long. How does the statue of Hygeia progress ? I know you must enjoy Calliope's studio, it is such a fascinating nook. I think with immense satisfaction of the friendship which must be growing between you two girls. You will do good, and get good from each other. Calliope is too intense ; she needs you to brighten and sweeten her life. [*Note by Phœbe.* — There, this covers me with shame and confusion. I shall go to see Calliope at once. To think that I have been a fortnight in Rome without going near her ! It is a burning shame !]

She has had some bitter disappointments. Some day, when you have won her confidence, you must get her to tell you about the gas-fixture man who engaged her to make a bronze candelabrum which was a great success, but who cunningly managed the business part so that she gained neither reputation nor money from it. The life of every artist is full of struggle. As I have been walking the streets of Florence, I have tried to think myself back to the year 1504, and to imagine the coming of Raphael, a young and unknown man, from the country town of Urbino to this great art centre. Leonardo da Vinci then was in the prime of his success, and Michael Angelo, lonely and gloomy, was battling with adverse fate. Here was lying Vasari, with no prophetic vision to foretell the fulsome praise which he would one day lavish on the world-accepted

THE MOSES OF MICHAEL ANGELO.

Raphael; crafty, two-faced Machiavelli; Fra Bartolommeo, the inspired artist monk; Cardinal Bibbiena, the jovial man of the world; and Bembo, a

> "Rose-i'-the-hat-rim Canon, cross at neck,
> And silk mask in the pocket of the gown."

I wonder what they all thought of the country youth and his new pictures. I can imagine one of his Madonnas or some other of his early pictures on private exhibition, and the Florentine connoisseurs and art critics filing by it with remarks not unlike those we hear nowadays; for art cant is as old as church cant. The first looker-on, who had not as yet heard the others give their opinion, might doubtfully mutter, "Not bad!" and crooking his hand into a funnel, eye the picture from a distance, waiting for some one else to break the ice. Then another, more courageous, obeying his natural instincts, might exclaim over the grace of composition and the exquisite sentiment of the picture, until some autocrat of the day poured cold water upon his enthusiasm by declaring the style "antiquated, servile imitation and affected sentimentality."

Next Machiavelli might cry, "When shall we have a national Art? Michael Angelo paints only athletes, and Perugino tells us his swollen muscles resemble a sack filled with walnuts; Da Vinci paints in twenty different styles; and here is this new adventurer desiring to introduce another manner."

Then an architect might admire the background, and announce himself a lover of the new science of perspective; and a poet would desire that a picture should be only vaguely suggestive of something mysterious and mystical. And so the procession troops by; one lamenting the lack of strength and realism, another wishing that it had been more decoratively treated, a third sighing for a modernly local stamp, and the rest praising and dispraising every several detail. I can imagine how Raphael closed his ears to the critics, both malicious and flattering, and worked out manfully his mission to cheer the heart and elevate the mind.

Michael Angelo seems to me, on the contrary, to have been affected by the gabble of tongues. Proud and sensitive, the iron entered into his soul; and though he fought bravely and overcame, something of the effort as well as the force of the wrestler is visible in all his works. I have no doubt that by this time you have been to see his "Moses." Tell me if the grand figure does not impress you as one who has conquered by force of will.

This is hardly telling you about Florence, but I remember that you were always fonder of people than of pictures. Just now the art world here is excited about some frauds perpetrated in one of the galleries. It seems that a picture by one of the old masters has been removed and a copy substituted. Detectives are now on the watch in London and Paris for the sale of the original picture. Every one wonders how the change could have been made, but the rogue will infallibly be discovered. The copy was recognized by the artist who executed it. I had a little conversation with him, and he told me that he had been painting on the copy a long time, and that he noticed a distinguished-looking stranger who frequently loitered through the galleries, seemed to take an interest in his work, and often paused behind him and watched his progress. When the painting was finished the stranger purchased it, paying with a check signed by Torlonia, the Roman banker. Of course the signature turned out to be a forgery, and shortly after the original picture disappeared and the copy was found in its place. It is a little extraordinary that the change was not immediately detected, for the canvas on which the picture was painted was slightly smaller than the original, it being a rule that no copies can be made of exactly the same size of any painting. The new canvas was artfully made to fit into the frame by the addition of a gold mat, and for several days it remained unnoticed.

The most alarming feature of it all to me is, that from the artist's description of the man who bought his picture, I believe him to be the Mr. Bartlett of whom I caught a glimpse in Venice, and who deceived us all so cleverly in Brazil under the name of Senhor Silva y Palacios. To think that this consummate rogue is wandering about Italy, perpetrating frauds upon confiding people, is enough to make one turn entirely from modern society and devote one's attention to the past.

Florence is full of the ghosts of the people who have lived here, some of them as rascally as our modern villains, and others who seem to us at this distance heroes and even saints.

The Medici take up the most room after the artists; from Lorenzo the Magnificent, who lifted his family to kingly power, and Giovanni, whom we know better as Pope Leo X., patron of arts and letters, to the fair and wicked women of that family who became queens of France, — Catherine, wife of Henry II., the unnatural mother, and Marie, queen of Henry IV.

After all, I am mistaken ; the earnest monk who stirred the hearts of all Florence with his fiery utterances, and refused Lorenzo absolution upon his death-bed unless he would give back liberty to the city, was grander than all the Medicis. It was under a damask rose-tree in the gardens of St. Mark that Savonarola began his preaching, where the Medicis had at great expense collected marvels of ancient art for the instruction of artists. Many of the artists

LEO X.

came to hear him, and were so moved by his eloquence that Fra Bartolommeo and others burned their pictures and gave themselves to the Church. For a time he swept all Florence with him. But the reaction came, and Savonarola was burned in the public square in 1498; and every March, when the anniversary comes round, the populace strew violets on the pavement. I have been re-

SAVONAROLA.

reading "Romola" and seeking out the localities which George Eliot mentions. I wandered about the Duomo, the grand cathedral which takes its name from its magnificent dome, the largest in the world.

Michael Angelo, when called to Rome to build St. Peter's, looked back upon it lovingly, and exclaimed, "Like it I will not, better I cannot." It is lighted by beautiful stained-glass windows, and without, standing isolated from the building, is the lovely Campanile.

> "And of all I saw and of all I praised,
> The most to praise and the best to see
> Was the startling bell-tower Giotto raised."

Slender and straight it is, — a lily of architecture.   They say that Giotto de-signed to have a flame-shaped spire on the summit; then, surely, it would have reminded one of a candle with aspiring, climbing flame.   As it is, it is a glori-ous candlestick, such as John in his vision might have seen set to represent the churches.   I paused long before the Ghiberti gates, the doors of the Bap-tistery, which Michael Angelo said were worthy to be the gates of Paradise ; and we came home over one of the bridges which span the Arno, and saw other bridges with their arches reflected in the glimmering water.   It was fairy-land. Afterward I took a little walk in the Loggia and bought a bit of Florentine mosaic, — only a trifle, a little pin with design of jasmine blossoms, but it will always recall to me the city of flowers, and my pleasant stay with this kind-hearted Florentine family.   A very unexpected circumstance has happened to me here.   I desired that some surgeon should examine Beatrice's hand, to assure the family that it had been properly treated.   They had spoken often of a Signor Steele — something, an Englishman in whom they had great confidence, but the

FRA GIUSEPPI.

name did not strike me as familiar ; and you may judge of my surprise when, after the examination, I was introduced to the Doctor Stillman whose skill and devotion saved the life of Professor Holmes on our South American journey.   He was as much as-tonished as I, for he had never heard of my studying medicine, and had declared that the child's accident had been skilfully treated.   He is an earnest, unassuming man, whom I thoroughly like ; and now that we have the same profession, we have a common interest.   He is watching the war-cloud which appears to be settling over Europe, and thinks of offering his services as surgeon to the English cause, and of hurrying away to Afghanistan.   I wish he could meet you and possibly he may ; for he talked inconsistently of Rome, as though it were on the way to the seat of war.

Yesterday we drove over the hills in the suburbs.   The villas glistened pale yellow and white among the green foliage, and the city lay below us a great flower garden, — the Duomo the rose, and the Campanile the lily, of the par-

CATHERINE DE' MEDICI.

terre. We drove to the Protestant cemetery just outside the Porta Pinta.
One might say of it as Keats did of the one at Rome where he and Shelley
lie buried, — that it would make one in love with death, to be buried in so
sweet a place. Nowhere else I have seen such beautiful box hedges. We

"FRA GIUSEPPI HAS LOST HIS NOSE."

found Mrs. Browning's grave, a sarcophagus of white marble, the only inscription, " E.B.B. Ob. 1861," and on the reverse, a lyre and a medallion. Theodore
Parker is also buried here.

But I shall see you so soon that it is not necessary for me to tell you of the
wonders of art at the Uffizi and Pitti palaces (the latter looks, from without,
like a penitentiary) ; of the "Venus de' Medici," Raphael's "Fornarina," and the
"Madonna della Seggiola ;" of the Palazzo Vecchio, Santa Croce, and the Convent
of St. Mark, with the frescos of Fra Angelico ; of Michael Angelo's statue of
"David" and Donatello's sculptures.

I have not said half enough of little Beatrice. She is a bright child with odd fancies, who likes to talk with grown people. One of her particular friends is a clerical gentleman, who visits often at the house, and whom we all call Fra Giuseppi. Her French governess was taking her to walk one day, I think in the Boboli Gardens, when Beatrice saw a statue which seemed to her to resemble Fra Giuseppi, with his little skull-cap and waving locks. But the statue had lost its nose, and Beatrice spied this slight defect at once. "Send for Dottore Vittoria," she cried, "quick, quick, to mend Fra Giuseppi's nose."

Were it not that the dear child still requires treatment, even beautiful Florence could not detain me, for I have an unaccountable feeling that you need me. You have not been ill or imprudent, I hope. Write a line to tell me that you are quite well, for if I were at all superstitious I should fancy that evil were lurking near you. On a spire which I can see from my window there is an iron weathercock shaped like a grotesque demon, and he points steadily toward Rome. Is the north wind giving me the megrims? From the Prince of the Power of the Air may all sweet influences fend you!

Lovingly always,

VICTORIA.

THE BAPTISTERY, DUOMO, AND CAMPANILE.

CHAPTER X.

"PLEASURES AND PALACES."

CALLIOPE'S STUDIO. — ST. PETER'S AND THE VATICAN.

VICTORIA's letter pricked my conscience, and I determined to call on Calliope at once. But I could not go to-day, for I had made an engagement with Count Torlonia to make the pilgrimage of the churches. We did not see the churches, after all, for the Count thought that the various palaces would be much more cheerful. Nat was busy over his lessons with Mr. Hathaway, so we formed just a carriage-full, — Aunt and the Count, Uncle Jonah and I. We drove first to the Barberini Palace. We passed a beautiful spiral stone staircase, and entered the picture-gallery, — a series of salons in which are many noted paintings. Guido's "Beatrice Cenci" I recognized at once, from the many copies that exist in America; but no copy can give the pathos of that face. There were other famous pictures by Raphael and Domenichino; but the sad eyes of Beatrice fascinated me, and I came back to her again and again.

We next paid a flying visit to the Rospigliosi Palace expressly for a peep at Guido's "Aurora." The painting is on the ceiling, but one does not have to tire one's neck by staring up at it, for a mirror is arranged upon a table, where one can see it reflected, and study every detail with perfect ease. "The Hours" were very beautiful, — some gay and hopeful, Hours yet to come, all radiant with the promise of the future; but one looks back with sad regret, as though thinking of "the tender grace of a day that is dead."

From the Rospigliosi we drove through the Piazza del Popolo to the Pincian Hill. It is the fashionable drive, and we passed and were passed by many gay equipages with liveried footmen and elegantly dressed women with soft Italian eyes. At the foot of the Pincian is a large square in the centre of which is an obelisk which the old Israelites looked upon in Egypt. Passing under Michael Angelo's gateway, we entered the Borghese grounds, lovely with artificial waterfalls fountains, and picturesque ruins so artfully constructed that one can hardly believe them manufactured for effect. Old sarcophagi, emptied for centuries of the dust they once held, served as ornaments. Beautiful trees and foliage plants of luxuriant growth, aloes and cacti and orange-trees, close-clipt lawns, and terraces set with statues, gladdened our city-tired eyes. One of those pure blue skies for which Italy is so praised relieved the yellow buildings, and the dark green of the old ilex-trees, the huge stone-pines

IN THE BORGHESE GARDENS.

and cypresses. Count Torlonia said that we should see a military review here, with all the brilliant panorama of gay uniforms, and the excitement of dashing manœuvres, and the fine music of an Italian band. But I could not imagine the scene lovelier than it was; nor did I regret when the Count ascertained that his friend the Prince Borghese was not at the villa. We visited afterward the Palazzo Borghese, and went through the picture-gallery,—twelve rooms. But it is hard to

PITTI PALACE.

study pictures when friends are chatting, and when one's perceptions are already sated, and I recall distinctly but two pictures. One is Raphael's "Entombment," which impressed me strongly; as much, I think, by the awe-inspiring majesty of Death in contrast with the gay and beautiful life all about us, as from the genius displayed in the painting. The other picture gave me a sudden surprise. I could hardly believe at first that it was not a portrait of Count Torlonia, so strongly did it resemble him; there was the same aristocratic carriage of the head, the keen black eyes, and handsome mouth. To be sure, the costume was not of to-day, but he might have chosen this picturesque mediæval dress for its pictorial effect. But Count Torlonia declared that he had never sat for his portrait, and did not appear pleased that we should all have been struck with the resemblance. We turned to our catalogues and found that it was a portrait of Cæsar Borgia. I studied the painting again, and the pleasurable feeling which I at first experienced faded away, for I could see that the eyes were secret and evil. Mrs. Hawthorne says that they reminded her of the eyes of a sullen vulture, — "vicious and designing, and above all, cold and indifferent." Strange to say, as I compared them I saw the same look in the eyes of the Count. He was looking at the portrait with a set scowl; but it lasted only a moment and he burst into light laughter, avowed himself complimented, and only wished that he were really as handsome.

Aunt Pen protested against seeing any more picture-galleries, and we drove to a pleasant restaurant on the Corso, and dined to the accompaniment of pleasant music. Then we were quite ready for home; but the Count insisted on taking us along the Ripetta, and past St. Peter's Church to the Vatican Palace.

A glorious sunset was flinging its splendors across the sky, and we were glad to stroll in the Pope's beautiful garden, with no thought of lifting our tired minds up to the point of appreciating masterpieces. The high hedges which divide the grounds into fanciful labyrinths were capital places for a recluse to pace with his breviary, — a still

kinder solitude for two, the Count said. During the sixteenth century, in the days of old Leo X., the gardens resounded with music
and the laughter of fair women. It is a charming spot; and the only
puzzle was to tell which was the more delicious, this or the Villa
Pamfili Doria, which we saw a little later, its stately façade lighted by
a full-orbed Italian moon. Another name for the villa is Belrespiro.
We rode about the avenues, passing from mysterious shade into sheets
of silver light, and startling the pheasants in the shrubbery. We
admired the beautiful view of St. Peter's and the Campagna. As we
left the grounds a spray of ivy was caught by a wheel of the carriage
and thrown into my lap, and I have kept it as a souvenir.

CALLIOPE'S STUDIO.

An excursion is planned for to-morrow; and so after our late
breakfast this morning, though Aunt Pen tried to persuade me that I
ought to stay at home to-day and rest, I determined not to let another
day go by without finding Calliope Carter. She has called upon me,
but it was when we were all out; and I could never face Victoria and
tell her that I have not looked her up. Nat had already found her
studio, and thinking that I might have some difficulty, as it is in the
old portion of the city, he insisted on being my guide. Mr. Hathaway, too, took his hat and accompanied us. Calliope's studio is in
the queerest old caravansary I ever saw. Just behind the Capitol,
and fronting toward the Tiber, not far from the fish-market, stands
the ancient theatre of Marcellus, begun by Julius Cæsar, finished by
Augustus, and named for his nephew. It was built of Titanesque
blocks of stone somewhat in the style of the Coliseum, the lower story
ornamented with Doric columns, the second with Ionic, and the upper
with Corinthian. The building has fallen sadly from its ancient
grandeur; the great archways are filled in with inferior masonry, three
stories are crowded in the space originally occupied by one, and the

GARDENS OF THE VATICAN.

lower floor is an arcade of grimy little shops. Venders of charcoal,
of wine, vegetables, and second-hand merchandise, have established

REMAINS OF THE THEATRE OF MARCELLUS.

their depots here, and the entire neighborhood was malodorous in the
extreme. Nat pointed out one of the archways, which proved to be a
tunnel burrowing its way into the interior of the building; and Mr.
Hathaway said he would wait in a shop where there were some old

swinging church-lamps which interested him, until I had made my call. The interior of the theatre was very ruinous, but it contained a court where some stone-cutters were at work upon blocks of marble. Nat thought that one of them might be the piece from which the Hygeia was to be chiselled. We mounted a narrow staircase to the topmost story, till my breath forsook me and I clung panting to Nat. On the upper landing we found ourselves opposite a little door on whose green paint was scratched, — whittled, Nat said, — " C. Carter." Nat rang, and Calliope herself admitted us. She had on a great apron, and her fingers were coated with moist clay; but she embraced me all the same, and I did not mind it in the least. The interior of the apartment was as odd as its surroundings. It was lighted by a large studio window opening on the court, and was half sitting-room and half workshop. The sitting-room part was divided off by a wooden partition, boasted a large piece of carpet, and contained many little articles suggestive of feminine comfort, — a rocking-chair, a small desk, a bird-cage, and some flowering plants. But the studio proper was rigidly simple, even bare, with its great barrel of clay, a modelling-table, and, high on a shelf running around the wall, a quantity of plaster busts covered with a satin-like film of dust. Nat, having seen me safely in, descended once more, and left Calliope and me to our confidences. " How can you bear to live here all alone in this shock-ing quarter of Rome ? " I asked.

Calliope laughed. " This is a very aristocratic mansion, I assure you," she replied. " During the Middle Ages it was the fortress of the Pierleoni, the rivals of the Frangipani, who occupied the Coliseum. Later the Savelli palace was built upon and out of its ruins, and then it passed into the hands of the Orsini. In modern times it has been the residence of the historian Niebuhr. And then, I am not alone; I have a delightful girl for a chum, a Miss Finger from Cincinnati, who writes for the newspapers. Then right across the entry are the Weinbergers, whom I met first in Munich; the father is a scene-

VILLA PAMFILI DORIA.

painter, the son Carl a violinist in one of the orchestras here, and the girls are studying music. Carl is always ready to serve as escort if we need him; but Mrs. Clarke, of whom Victoria must have told you, is our mountain of strength in a social way. She sends her carriage for us and insists on having us at her pleasant evenings, and in

SLEEPING MODEL.

chaperoning us wherever a chaperone is required. But of course you are anxious to see your statue." Just then I was startled by a sneeze, and I noticed an old Italian woman fast asleep in a chair. "That is my model, — the Mother Aurelia," Calliope explained.

11

" Did she pose for Hygeia ? " I asked.

" Oh, no ! her grand-daughter, the pretty Octavia, posed for it. How do you like the design ? " So speaking, Calliope drew aside a

STATUES OF HYGEIA.

curtain and showed me the statue in clay.   I confess that I was a little disappointed at first at the dingy color and diminutive size; and

PORTICO OF OCTAVIA.

Calliope must have read my face, for she said, "You expected to see it in marble, did you not? And there has been plenty of time, but I have been unfortunate. The men chiselled it from this design in the court below, and when they had done I had the statue hoisted by a pulley, so that it could be swung through my studio window and I might myself do the finishing here. You see it was too large to come up the staircase as you did. There was a weak point in the mechanism somewhere; for when it was in mid-air the statue fell and shivered on the pavement below. It was very fortunate that no one was killed or injured."

"But what a loss to you!" I exclaimed. "You must let me pay for the extra labor of putting it in marble a second time."

"Indeed I cannot allow you to do so. You had not actually ordered the statue, and I had it put in marble feeling that I could dispose of it elsewhere if you did not care for it; besides, the loss is not so great as it might have been," Calliope replied, with a smile, "for an eccentric individual happened along the next day and bought a quantity of fragments of the stone-cutters, the Hygeia among other pieces. What he will do with the poor mutilated statue I am puzzled to imagine, for it resembled one of Garibaldi's veterans, or a genuine antique, in its armless and battered condition."

Calliope next brought out a quantity of photographs of different Hygeias. The one at the St. Petersburg Museum, with the serpent over her shoulder, is usually considered the most lovely; but I liked also the representation of the goddess at the Louvre, holding the cup in her left hand, with the snake coiling around her right arm. After all, Calliope's idea of the daughter of Æsculapius seemed to me the most pleasing. She is seated in a graceful classic pose, the snake is such a subordinate feature that it is not disagreeable, and the face is very lovely. Calliope has promised to have the pretty model come sometime and take the position for Victoria and me.

"Where are you going now?" she asked, as I was leaving. And ascertaining that we were on our way to

ST. PETER'S AND THE VATICAN,

she kindly dismissed her model and accompanied us.

"I want to show you my favorite statue," she said — "Michael Angelo's ' Pietà,' and I would like also to see how you are impressed by the greatest and most magnificent of all churches." Before crossing the Tiber we wandered through the fish-market, which is held under the Portico of Octavia, near Calliope's quarters, and really one of the most picturesque nooks in Rome, contrasting as it does the ancient ruins with the life of the common people. I think Mr. Hathaway did not notice anything peculiar in Calliope; but to me her quiet independence and utter disregard of conventionality is a little shocking, though I could not help admiring the conscious rectitude which was so fearless of misconstruction.

We crossed the Tiber, and shortly after found ourselves in front of St. Peter's. The two great colonnades reached out their embracing arms about the obelisk and the two flashing fountains. Passing through the vestibule, we pushed aside the heavy curtain and entered the twilight of the church. It did not impress me at first as immense. It was only after I had walked about and compared distances, and discovered how long it took me to reach an object which seemed quite near, that I realized the grand scale upon which it is constructed.

The plan of the church is a Latin cross. The altar is in the centre, covered by a canopy which would seem high were it not precisely under the great dome. Outside of its colossal proportions, the glory of St. Peter's lies in its mosaics. The floor, the walls, the ceiling, the pictures over the altars, are all executed in this marvellous way. Calliope led us to the chapel containing the " Pietà." It is a statue of the dead Christ in the arms of his mother. I did not care particularly for the Christ, though it is unquestionably a dead body, the torture-racked limbs hanging limp and nerveless; but the Madonna is full of

womanly dignity, and above all, of tender motherhood. She has taken
the corpse upon her knee, as though her dear son were a little boy

PIETÀ.

once more, and holds him close to her breast with such a loving em-
brace that if the Catholics had never before worshipped Mary, it

would not seem strange that this expression of divine mother-love should have won them to adoration.

Mr. Hathaway and Nat climbed to the roof, but I was content to rest. I wish I might have seen an illumination of St. Peter's, when the great Bengal lights burn, and the torch-bearers run along the roof outlining its shape by lighting hundreds of lamps.

We passed from the church to the long galleries of the Vatican, which give one an idea of Papal magnificence, and whose long array of marbles and pictures tired me wofully. Calliope pointed out the "St. Jerome of Domenichino," which she said was one of the ten great pictures of the world, and the "Madonna da Folignio," a very lovely Raphael; but the picture which interested me most was his last painting, "The Transfiguration," which stood in his studio unfinished on that Easter Day, 1520, when Rome passed by in sad procession, and looked, not at the picture, but at the dead face of their idolized painter lying upon his bier beneath it.

Raphael was an indefatigable worker, and his decorations in the Vatican prove how conscientiously he finished even to the minutest detail. The painter who could unroll heavenly visions on great canvases seemed to take an exquisite pleasure in depicting the gambols of tiny field-mice and the graceful foliations of the Renaissance conventional ornament.

We entered the Sistine Chapel to study Michael Angelo's frescos, his grand Sibyls and Prophets; and quite unexpectedly we heard part of an exquisite chant, for the choir were practising. Calliope likes my plan of visiting the different churches, and has promised to take me next week. Some way I have a feeling that she is more reliable than our charming friend the Count, and I believe we shall really accomplish this long-cherished plan.

CHAPTER XI.

AN EXCURSION TO TIVOLI AND A PILGRIMAGE OF THE CHURCHES.

WE had heard that there was to be a peasant's fair at Tivoli, and the Count urged our attending it, as it would afford us an opportunity of observing the peasantry, over whose picturesqueness he became very enthusiastic; and really the day has brought us nearer to the life of the common people of modern Italy than all our other sight-seeing. I do not think the Count cares greatly for close contact with the peasantry, but prefers to appreciate their pictorial aspects from a distance. All along the road we overtook and passed straggling groups of queer people trooping to the fair.

A blind organ-grinder leaned against a post by the wayside and ground patriotic airs, sadly out of tune, from a small box, and asked alms in the name of the Madonna. Women trudged along in their holiday costume, adorned with immense silver ear-rings and many chains. Some carried on their heads jars of honey or great bags of chestnuts to sell or exchange for trinkets; all had a gay, expectant air, in contrast with the weary dulness of the Campagna road over which they were passing. The plain seemed only more desolate for the ruins of aqueducts and baths with which

it was dotted here and there. Tivoli is about twenty miles from Rome.
It is a very old town, — four hundred years older than Rome, Mr.
Hathaway said, and the residence of Zenobia, of Horace, and of Cassius and Brutus.   But if Tivoli were as young as one of our Western
American cities, it would still have attractions enough in the beauty

of its situation. Its modern villas
and ancient ruins cling to the cliffs
of Monte Ripoli, while the Sabine
Mountains form a natural amphitheatre around it.   The River Anio
dashes through it, and falling over a
precipice forms the celebrated cas-
cade.   As far as the eye can make
out architectural forms, one can
recognize the small round temple of
Vesta, the Sibyl, or Hercules (for
authorities give it different names),
perched above the falls on the very
edge of a sheer descent.   A railing
has been placed at its foot, and later
in the day we examined it closely,
and picked up some party-colored
marbles, fragments of an old mosaic,
as souvenirs.

BLIND ORGAN-GRINDER.

I learn from Bayard Taylor's
Travels that the Cascatelles (or cas-
cades) are formed by that part of the Anio which is used in the iron-
works made out of the ruins of Mecænas's villa; and not far distant are
the remains of the villa of Horace.

The fair was a Babel.   Booths were erected in the market-place ;
and ham, legs of bacon, cheese, toys, religious ornaments, scarfs,
cakes, and gay umbrellas tempted the natives.   Graceful flasks of

TIVOLI.

white and red wine were offered for sixteen cents. Strolling moun-
tebanks amused the crowd, while in a shady grove the young people
were dancing the Tarantella, and the more aged thronged the church,
which was decorated with fresh paper flowers and an illumination of
candles, recalling still another of Browning's poems : —

> " Not a post nor a pillar but 's dizened
> With red and blue papers ;
> All the roof waves with ribbons, each altar 's
> Ablaze with long tapers.
> And there will the flaxen-wigged Image
> Be carried in pomp
> Through the plain, while in gallant procession
> The priests mean to stomp.
> And all round the glad church lie old bottles
> With gunpowder stopped,
> Which will be, when the Image re-enters,
> Religiously popped."

We picnicked in the beautiful grounds of Villa d' Este, and then
returned to Rome by way of Frascati, passing by other lovely villa-
crowned slopes, and dark-eyed Italian girls handsome enough to have
served as models to Raphael.

As the sun sank we could see the hills lighted up with fire-
works and great bonfires. Aunt Pen was afraid of the malaria of the
Campagna, and urged the coachman to drive faster. I fastened my
cloak more tightly at the throat, and she noticed that my hands were
bare. " Put on your gloves, child," she exclaimed ; and I was obliged
to confess that I had lost them, as I thought, at the Villa d' Este.
But the Count drew them from his pocket, saying that he had found
them, and had taken the liberty to take charge of them until I should
claim my property. I put them on at once, and as I did so felt something cold slip over one of my fingers. A ring had been placed inside,
and quite unwittingly I had put it on ! The Count sat opposite, regarding me with a quiet smile which recalled our conversation in the

Catacombs. I could not create a scene by giving him back the ring then and there, but I took off the glove as quickly as if there had been a spider inside it. The Count looked away and said nothing. Now

TEMPLE OF HERCULES.

that I am at home and alone, the ring lies beside me. It is the one with the coin as a signet bearing the device of a man contending with a lion. I shall never wear it, or accept any present, however trivial,

TEMPLE OF VESTA.

from the Count again. I have placed it inside the Borgia glass until I shall have an opportunity to return it. If it retains its virtue of

THE WINE-SELLER.

detecting the presence of evil, the glass will guard or at least warn me of any danger. I wonder whether this is the mysterious influence which Victoria dreaded.

Heigh-ho! I wish she were here.

A PILGRIMAGE OF THE CHURCHES.

I have not written of our Sundays in Rome, because we have not devoted them to sight-seeing. I have not even gone to any of the great show churches on Sunday, because I could not do so with any

spark of religious feeling. We attended service usually at the Protestant Chapel, or went where there was preaching in French, which
we understand better than Italian.

There are so many churches in Rome! It seems a city of churches
and palaces, and they are scattered in every quarter, so that nowhere
does one get beyond the sound of church-bells. Nat says that they
divide the hours of the day and night between them, so that at no
time, from Angelus to Vespers and from Vespers to Angelus, is there
a moment when the clangor of bells entirely ceases. Except among
the ruins, it is always noisy in Rome.

> " Ere opening your eyes in the city the blessed church-bells begin ;
> No sooner the bells leave off, than the diligence rattles in."

Calliope said it would be useless for us to attempt to visit more
than four or five of the principal ones, and suggested that we should
begin with the Basilica of Santa Maria Maggiore.

I asked her the meaning of the word " basilica," and she explained
that it was the Roman court-house, which in country towns served
also as market-place. Many of these basilicas were converted into
Christian churches with very little change in the architecture, for
aisles ran down the length of the building furnished with galleries,
which were the lounging-places of the spectators. The judge's seat
occupied a semicircular recess at the end opposite the entrance, where
the altar now stands. St. Peter's is the principal Roman basilica.
Santa Maria Maggiore is also a basilica, and one of the oldest churches
in the city. It would be difficult with mere pen and paper to give an
idea of its magnificence, — the many-colored marbles in the mosaics
and pillars, the lavish use of gold and precious stones, the works of
sculpture and costly canvases with which it abounds ; and an artist's
brush would be required to give the effect which greeted us as we
entered from the dull gray light of a cloudy day into the twinkling
illumination of hundreds of candles. The Princess Borghese — Lady

VILLA D' ESTE.

Gwendoline Talbot, of English birth and parentage — is buried here. She was greatly beloved by the poor of Rome, to whom she was very kind, and they attended her funeral weeping bitterly. It is said that her gentle ghost haunts the church. Never before have I felt the slightest attraction to a life of rank and wealth, and it comes to me

AT SANTA MARIA MAGGIORE.

now, not from the palaces, but from the homes of the poor; not for the wider opportunity it would give me as a society leader, but for the sake of being loved as this woman was loved, for her deeds of charity.

Some miserable-looking beggars were kneeling on the mosaic floor side by side with an elegantly clothed woman, — a lady of rank, as I afterward learned, — and the sight gave me a lesson seldom taught in our American churches.

We left the great Church of St. John of Lateran, with its palace, on the site of the residence of so many popes, and the staircase up which Luther climbed upon his knees, for another day, and passed on.

to St. Paul's, beyond the walls. It is one of the simplest yet most
palatial of churches. Its highly polished marble floor reflects every
object, and gives one the sensation of walking upon mirrors. It
would have made a beautiful ball-room, I could not help thinking, for
the very richness took away any feeling of reverence. Unlike most
Roman churches, it was well lighted. Eighty marble pillars flanked
the great hall, and over them were set circular medallions, portraits in
mosaic of all the popes.

Mr. Hathaway prefers the old Gothic cathedrals of the north, and
says that in Rome Christianity still suffers from having been grafted
on a pagan stock. The most disagreeable of all the shrines of our
pilgrimage was the Church of the Capuchins, in spite of its fine Guido
Reni, "St. Michael overthrowing the Devil;" for here are the ghastly
crypts filled with the bones of monks. The vaults of this church are
paved with earth brought from the Holy Land, in which it is the privilege of the clerical orders to be buried; but as the graves are limited
in number, when once filled the oldest inhabitant has to be exhumed
to make room for the next comer. The bones of the displaced monks
ornament the sepulchral chambers, sorted and arranged in fantastic
designs, spinal columns and scapulas worked up into lamps, and
niches constructed of skulls, in which entire skeletons were arranged
as statues, robed in the dress of their order. It was altogether the
most frightful chamber of horrors I ever entered, and one which I
fear will long haunt my dreams. I was glad to breathe the outer air
once more, and to get away from the influences of the grewsome
place.

The churches which I enjoyed most were not the exhibition buildings, where priests in "custard-colored gowns" marked with cherry-
tart crosses made what Channing calls "a great fumigation," but the
more obscure and out-of-the-way places which we happened upon, and
did not find set down in the guide-book. There was one where we
heard some nuns sing through a grating, which may have been the

ST. PAUL BASILICA.

same chapel where Mendelssohn loved to attend vespers, and for whose nuns he composed a *Miserere*, or some other piece of sacred music. Mrs. Jameson seems to share the same feeling, and says : " For myself, I know nothing to compare with a pilgrimage among the antique churches scattered over the Cælian and the Aventine Hills. They stand apart, each in its solitude, amid gardens and vineyards and heaps of nameless ruins : here a group of cypresses, there a lofty pine or solitary palm; the tutelary saint, perhaps some San Achilleo or Santa Bibiana, whom we never heard of before, columns of porphyry, the old frescos dropping from the walls, the everlasting colossal mosaics looking down so solemn, so dim, so spectral : these grow upon us until they may be said to hallow our daily life — when considered in a right spirit."

We found one of Mrs. Jameson's favorite churches, San Clemente, on the road leading from the Coliseum to the Lateran. Clement was third bishop of Rome. St. Paul alludes to him in Philippians iv. 3, — " Clement also, and other my fellow-laborers whose names are written in the book of life." Mrs. Jameson gives the legend of St. Clement, explaining the anchor which is usually represented with him as his emblem. The church is a very interesting one, consisting of three stories, two of them underground, discovered at different times. It is considered a fine example of the ancient basilica.

The most flagrant instance of image-worship we found at the Church of Santa Maria in Araceli, which we reached by a flight of one hundred very tiresome steps. It is built on the ruins of an old Roman temple, and is in charge of Franciscan monks, who make no small income by the exhibition of " Il santo Bambino," — an ancient doll made of olive-wood, representing the Christ child, and wrapped in costly swaddling clothes. This idol — for such it really is — was formerly sent to visit sick people ; is supposed to have performed many miracles of healing, and is a popular object of adoration. It is shown to the public on the festival of Epiphany, and is as hideous an object in its way as an ancient Hindu deity. One wonders that among such beautiful creations of art the representations of the Virgin and Child, which are most popular, should be so ugly.

> " Noon strikes ; here sweeps the procession, our Lady borne smiling and smart,
> With a pink gauze gown all spangles, and seven swords stuck in her heart."

Take it as a whole, my little tour of the churches has been a disheartening one. If any one is inclined toward Romanism by the eloquent preaching of such a propagandist as Monsignor Capel, I advise her to come to Rome, and I believe that the result will be, as in the case of Luther, a complete disillusion. Of the churches that were on our list that we did not see, are the Gesu or magnificent edifice of the Jesuits, San Pietro in Vincoli, and Santa Maria Sopra Minerva; but I have seen enough and more than enough, and shall not try again.

All through the day a new idea has been moving in my brain. The ring which I left last night in the Borgia glass means a villa at Rome, an opportunity such as the Princess Borghese had for doing good. Can I throw it aside out of mere personal whim? Is it not a thing to be seriously considered? If one could only surely know whether it were a leading of Providence or a temptation of the Evil One. A strange thing has just happened. I went to my toilet-table to look at the ring, and found the Venetian glass in fragments. What does it mean? Was there a grain of the Borgia poison hidden in the ring, which has acted chemically upon the glass? Or had the cup the power of detecting still more subtle influences, and is this a warning of something malignant and deadly threatening me through this little ring? Or, again, was it the merest chance,—a puff of air from the open window, a whisk of the plumy tail of Aunt Pen's Angora cat, Henri of Navarre?

I'll leave the questions to Victoria.

SAN CLEMENTE.

CHAPTER XII.

VICTORIA has come. I have told her everything, and I can see that she is troubled. The mere telling has settled the matter for me, and I wonder how I could ever have hesitated. I have sent the ring back to the Count by Nat, and we are going to Calliope's studio to see the pretty model pose for my statue.[1]

We have returned after a delightful hour. The model was gracefully draped in the Greek costume, and held a very natural jointed toy snake. I long to see the statue on its pedestal in the new gymnasium. Calliope herself, in her modelling costume, was the personification of health and energy.

Nat has come in, bringing a note from the Count. He has been called suddenly to his villa at Baiæ, near Naples. As he knows that we are going south soon, he hopes to see us there and to show us the wonderful statues which have been found upon his estate. Baiæ was a famous Roman watering-place, and there were many summer palaces here in the most luxurious period of the ancient times, and it is not to be wondered at that beautiful remains should be found upon this spot. Uncle Jonah is sure that I will change my mind about Calliope's Hygeia as soon as I have seen the Count's discoveries.

Victoria laughingly wonders whether the Count is not a magician or a ghost, since he always vanishes whenever she appears. She pretends to doubt his existence, and that he is a little fiction which we have all arranged as a sort of Marjorie Daw hoax.

[1] See frontispiece.

The Mr. Bartlett of whom she wrote me from Florence has been traced to Rome. It seems that he is a member of a band of forgers who have been creating dismay among bankers by presenting false letters of credit, and obtaining large sums in other fraudulent ways.

There are rumors of cholera in the East, and Uncle thinks we had better hasten our visit to Naples while it is still winter. I am reluctant to leave Rome; for we have been very happy here, and yet we have seen no society, have attended no receptions, have made no acquaintances. I could never have believed such an existence endurable ; but I am stronger, less nervous, weigh more, and can walk farther than when we came.

My journal reads like a guide-book, with its enumeration of the places we have visited; and yet we have not seen half of the remarkable objects in this wonderful city.

We have been down to the Fountain Trevi for a farewell draught, for there is a tradition that those who drink of its waters will return again to Rome. In response to our good-by toast Mr. Hathaway repeated Channing's

FAREWELL.

Farewell to Rome ! farewell, ye ruins high,
Whose shattered arches float against the sky ;
Farewell, ye giant Baths where grandeur dwells ;
Farewell, beneath the ground, the Martyrs' cells ;
Thou Rome art centred in my inmost heart,
Palace of Kings, great storehouse of fine art,
Where Virgil sang his mellow summer hymn,
Where Caesar made all lesser fortunes dim,
Where Raphael with his pencil moulded men,
Where Michael with his chisel lived again. —
Farewell ! farewell forever to thee Rome !
Fade the last circles of thy mountain dome,
Through rosy twilight's intermingling ray, —
Farewell to thee, farewell the Southern day.

ROCK OF TERRACINA.

We have decided to make the journey to Naples by carriage along the sea-coast, on the old Appian Way. The railroad lies more to inland, and passes over a comparatively uninteresting country.

We have passed over the Pontine Marshes with their history of death, have passed a night at Terracina and viewed the ruins, and have put our four-in-hand to their best paces through Itri; for Itri is the heart of the brigand region. Nat wanted to stop here and " scare up an adventure ;" but the glimpse we caught of the village of women with no men anywhere visible was not encouraging. Many of the women were beautiful, and even the hags wore gay-colored rags which made bright spots of blue and orange and crimson in the picture ; but where were the men ? Off in the mountains, possibly, with some bandit chief, waiting to be informed of the approach of just such travellers as we. We paused at Gaeta, smothered with citrons and acacias. Then a night at Capua and more ruins, and here we are at Naples.

Yes, it is really Naples, its houses rising like the seats of an amphitheatre around the arena of the bay. The islands of Ischia and Capri tip the two points of the beautiful crescent, and Mount Vesuvius, like an old Indian sachem, sits wrapped in his gray mantle of lava, smoking his pipe in the background. All along the sweep of shore we can discern nestling villages — Pozzuoli off to the right, and Baiæ is somewhere in that direction, where the Count has his villa and statues; and away to the left, following the trend of the coast, are Torre del Greco at the foot of Vesuvius, Castellamare with its fishing-boats, and Sorrento in the distance. Naples itself, whether we drive along the Toledo — a street of palaces — or climb the precipitous little lanes that go wander-

ing up and down broken stairways, is a most interesting city. I never tire of the street life, and have been about a good deal. I like walking

BRONZE TRIPOD FROM POMPEII.

best, and these before-mentioned steep streets, which have no wheel-ruts, and are only footpaths for people and donkeys. It is amusing to

NAPLES AND MOUNT VESUVIUS.

watch the milkmen drive their herds of goats from door to door, milk-
ing the required amount into the pitchers which the maids hand them,
with no opportunity of adulterating
the milk.   Victoria and I have refreshed ourselves with orangeade
mixed with mountain snow, which
we purchased at little booths on
the street, and we have watched
the expressive pantomime of the
fishermen and fish-women as they
quarrel over their wares.   A great
deal of small business is done
upon the street.   We noticed a
little boy doing a thriving trade
in cast-away cigar-stumps, which
he displayed upon the sidewalk
and sold to other urchins.

     We have been to the Museum
as a matter of duty.   A little of
the laziness of this soft southern
air creeps into one's veins and
makes it difficult to do anything
which requires exertion, though
we have climbed to the Castle of
St. Elmo, and to the Church of
San Martino, the richest in Naples, which crown the heights.
But that was in the first days of
our residence.   We have been
here a week now, and are old

VENUS OF CAPUA.

Neapolitans.   The Museum was a weariness of the flesh, with its
Pompeian antiquities.   If one could see only the best, without being

obliged to look at everything. Some of the statues were very beautiful. The Venus of Capua is remarkably so, and we were struck by a Satyr carrying a baby Bacchus on his shoulder; but for restful pleasure there is nothing like a walk in the Villa Reale, a beautiful garden thrown open to the public, with its tropical palms, its flowers and fountains tempting you ever a little farther. While loitering here one day we noticed a man taking photographs. "That is an American," I exclaimed; "every motion proclaims the fact." But as we passed him we saw that he had the long hair and dark complexion of an Italian, and I saw that I was mistaken. He gave a little start as Victoria passed him, as though he recognized her, but he seemed to change his mind, for he thrust his head almost instantly under the black cloth that draped his camera. He seemed to be taking photographs of the passers-by rather than of the scenery, — a circumstance which seemed to me a little odd.

POMPEII.

We have returned from an excursion to the city which Bulwer has made alive to us all. We took the cars early in the morning and passed through Resina, the station which one leaves for the ascent of Vesuvius. Victoria, Mr. Hathaway, and Nat will make this trip a little later; but Aunt Pen, Uncle Jonah, and I feel too old for such a fatiguing jaunt. Torre del Greco was the next station, still under the skirts of the volcano. It seems strange that people will insist on living there, for whenever there is an eruption the town is in danger. The inhabitants have a proverb, *Napoli fa i peccati e la Torre li paga*, — "Naples sins and the Torre suffers;" so whenever Naples is more than usually depraved this poor little village expects chastisement. At the next Torre we struck away from the sea for the buried city. We entered by the Street of Graves. I think that the dead Pompeians whose ashes were quietly resting in their urns were more to be envied

STREET OF GRAVES.

on that awful night of the first eruption than the living. How strange it was to be able to wander from street to street, the pavement cut with chariot-wheels and the walls marked with the business and political announcements of the day, — to stroll unhindered through the

DEALER IN LOVES (FROM AN ANTIQUE FRESCO).

apartments of the wealthy and the mysterious chambers of the temples of Isis and of Venus! We walked across the fields to the arena, — a mere baby affair after the Coliseum, and much too small for the elaborate programme which Bulwer supposes to have been enacted here ; and yet, though Bulwer may not be archæologically correct, it is he who has made us realize the luxurious life that went out in that great horror of darkness. It is of Nidia and Glaucus that one thinks ;

and we do not inquire with nearly as much interest for Sallust and
Pansa and the Tragic Poet, whose houses were pointed out to us by the
guide. At the latter was found a mosaic representing a dog, beneath
which was the inscription, *Cave Canem,* — "Beware of the dog!"

Some of the mosaics were beautiful, but more were simply curious,
and made you wonder at the toil by which they were constructed.
The frescos were graceful and fanciful, many of them exquisitely
lovely. Venus and Cupids the favorite subjects, as though life were
all love and beauty, and then, in awful contrast, those hollow moulds
left by the forms of those who died on that fatal day, which have since
been filled with plaster, and show to the minutest detail the death-
agony of these poor creatures. We all agreed that it was the most
impressive sermon we had ever attended. Mr. Howells, it seems to
me, best describes Pompeii in its present state. He says: —

"What is it comes to me at this distance of that which I saw at Pompeii?
The narrow and curving but not crooked streets, with the blazing sun falling
into them; the houses, and the gay columns of white, yellow, and red; the
delicate pavements of mosaic; inanimate garden spaces with pygmy statues
suited to their littleness; suites of fairy bed-chambers painted with exquisite
frescos; dining-halls with joyous scenes of hunt and banquet on their walls;
the ruinous sites of temples; the lonesome tragic theatre; the baths with their
roofs perfect yet, and the stucco bas-reliefs all but unharmed; around the whole
the city wall crowned with slender poplars; outside the gates the long avenue
of tombs, and in the distance Vesuvius, brown and bare, with his fiery breath
scarce visible against the cloudless heaven, — these are the things that float
before my fancy as I turn back to look at myself walking those enchanted
streets, and to wonder if I could ever have been so blest."

At Pompeii we saw the same American-looking photographer.
This time he had no tripod, but carried a small hand-bag which
Victoria thought was a sneak-box, or concealed camera arranged for
taking instantaneous photographs. He prowled about, regarding the
ruins with an uninterested air as though he were looking for some
person, and did not in the least care for the beauties of art by which

he was surrounded. Nat said he had a hungry air, and was in search of one of the Pompeian bakers, and looked his disappointment at not finding him at home.

Uncle Jonah is impatient to go to Baiæ and have the matter of the statue decided. We found the Count's card at the hotel with some

THE TEMPLE OF ISIS.

exquisite flowers after our return from Pompeii, and a line urging us to set a day for our excursion. I dread to go, and mean to put it off as long as I can ; but Uncle has heard that there really are a few cases of cholera here, and is anxious to hurry things. However, we want to see Capri too, and have decided to make the southern excursion first.

CHAPTER XIII.

Mr. HATHAWAY suggested that we ought to stop at Portici and see the remains of Herculaneum; but Uncle and Nat were sure that the best of everything found there had been removed to the Museum at Naples, and we sped away over the same road that we took yesterday, past the two Torres, and through Castellamare to Sorrento. We are stopping at the Albergo del Tasso, so named in honor of the poet. who was born in this place in 1544. I had brought Mrs. Stowe's "Agnes of Sorrento" to serve as our guide-book, and we have spent the afternoon in looking up the places mentioned, — the mysterious gorge, with the "Dovecot" hidden under the orange-trees where Agnes lived; the Capuchin convent, on whose flat roof Padre Francesco paced; and the cloisters of St. Agnes on the cliffs. Of course the story is only a pretty fiction, but it is delightfully true to nature. The view from the heights away toward the blue sea is enchanting, and on the other side of the headland we know that beautiful Amalfi nestles, and farther on is Salerno.

And now we have returned to Naples, and in half an hour I must tell how we took a boat to Capri, ate delicious fish, and read from Hans Christian Andersen's "Improvisatore," to prepare us for the Blue Grotto, which we did not see until the next day, for the tide was not right. We consoled ourselves for our disappointment by a

BRIDGE AT SORRENTO.

donkey-ride up the cliffs to the ruins of the Villa of Tiberius, where we obtained entrancing views and endeavored to feel a befitting horror at the villany of the old emperor. Our guide had a fine voice, and sang " Dolce Napoli " patiently and good-humoredly to our repeated *encores*. We reached the Blue Grotto the next morning by boat. In order to enter we were obliged to lie down or crouch very low, while a friendly swell of the great rollers swept us under the low arch. The light within is bluish and spectral, but we hardly experienced the same transports which Hans Andersen describes so graphically. The landlord, on our return to the inn, endeavored to keep us a day longer in Capri to see a Green Grotto on the other side of the island; but Aunt Pen was anxious about her dogs, which had been left at Naples, and we returned to Sorrento. Giovanni, our guide, whose fine voice we had all admired, told us that he had a brother who was a musician in America, who was fast becoming rich. Victoria became greatly interested, and named over the different tenors whom Colonel Mapleson has brought out. " Was it Galassi or possibly Campanini ? " But no; his brother was not a singer, only a musician. We had some difficulty in understanding the name of the instrument on which he had won such golden opinions, but it finally proved to be a hand-organ!

At Sorrento we took a carriage and drove along the crest of the cliffs to Amalfi, as it seems to me the loveliest drive in all the world. From Amalfi we continued our drive to Salerno, where we spent the night, and devoted the next day to the ruins of the Temples of Neptune and Ceres at Pæstum. The great Doric columns of travertine are wonderfully perfect and fresh-looking, and yet they are the conundrum of antiquaries. No one knows when or by whom they were built.

> " Time was they stood along the crowded street,
> Temples of gods ! And on their ample steps
> What various habits, various tongues beset
> The brazen gates for prayer and sacrifice."

14

At first the place seemed very desolate, only a few goats browsing among the ruins; but presently we discovered our friend the photographer wandering about the fields. Nat calls him our ghost, for he seems to dog our footsteps; and yet whenever he sees us he moves quietly away. This time, strange to say, Victoria has an impression that she has met him somewhere in America.

From Salerno we returned by rail to Naples, a rather odd thing happening at the station. Mr. Hathaway's hand-bag is an ordinary black one, and he exchanged it for another, exactly similar, belonging to one of our fellow-passengers. On opening it, the peaceful little clergyman was much surprised at being confronted by a pair of Colt's revolvers. Our first impression was that he had unwittingly possessed himself of the baggage of a duelling party; but as he dived farther into the mysterious recesses of the little bag he discovered a pair of handcuffs, which startled and puzzled us even more than the pistols had done. There was no clew whatever by which he could return the property, though its owner is probably in Naples. He ought, however, to hear soon from his own bag, for it contained a copy of the revised version of the New Testament bearing his name in full, and some letter-paper with the mark of our hotel.

AN AMERICAN NEWSPAPER.

CAPRI.

A package of American newspapers has just been sent up from the banker's, the first news we have received from home since leaving Rome, and Uncle is greatly excited over one item of news.

It has been proved, by the confession of one of his accomplices, that the man who stole the Florentine painting is the Mr. Bartlett whom Victoria suspected all the time. He has committed a number of frauds in the line of art. One of his schemes has been to supply archæological societies and museums of sculpture with false antiquities. It is said that he has a factory of forgeries of this kind in the neighborhood of Naples, and that detectives have been sent out to apprehend him.

It is all clear to Victoria now; she is positive that the photographer is a Mr. Jenkins, a detective, whom she met in South America, where he was searching for this same Mr. Bartlett, and she hopes that he will be more successful this time. I wonder whether we have met the forger, and in what disguise. Victoria has given me a very particular description of his appearance; but she says he is so clever in disguising himself that it is doubtful whether I, or even she, would recognize him.

We have had a beautiful Sabbath, and have attended the English service. The Protestants in Naples have united in establishing charity schools, in which Mr. Hathaway is much interested; he will visit them to-morrow, while the rest of our party make by carriage the dreaded excursion to Baiæ. I know that Uncle will want me to take the Count's statue instead of Calliope's, and I dislike to oppose Uncle's wishes, especially as he is so kind as to purchase it for me. But this is my first opportunity of being a patroness, and in all future decisions of this kind I intend to let merit alone decide, with a possible tipping of the scale toward the one who needs patronage most, provided the merit is equal. As a society woman I shall doubtless find myself in difficult situations, where it will be my business to interest and influence people in the right direction, to rouse enthusiasm where none exists, and carry unpopular movements by a large majority; but then Uncle Jonah is a particularly knotty specimen to begin upon. Nat is on my side. He is sure that the antique statue will prove to be a broken-nosed old monstrosity not in any way comparable with our exquisite Hygeia, which unfortunately Uncle has not seen. Victoria seems unusually impatient. "At last," she says, "I am to see this remarkably shy Count, who always flies at my approach."

Evening. Our drive has been a delightful one, and the further experiences somewhat startling.

> " A glory of oleander bloom
> Borders every bend of the craggy road ;
> The lemon and spice tree with rare perfume
> The lingering cloud-fleets heavily load :
> And over the beauty and over the balm
> Rises the crown of the royal palm."

Our route took us through the Grotto of Posilippo, a very long tunnel damp with little trickling streams, but lighted by lamps. Just above it, in a vegetable garden, is the tomb of Virgil, which bears out the comparison that Mr. Howells made to a sunken spring-house, — a thought which he well says would not have offended the poet, who loved and sang of humble country things. The walls were adorned with many scribblings. Nat copied this inscription in his note-book :

> " Qui cineres? tumuli hæc vestigia conditur olim
> Ille hic qui cecinit pascua, rura, duces."

We followed the curving beach to Pozzuoli, where St. Paul landed, and where there are ruins of temples. The ground here is volcanic. Monte Nuovo, a large hill which we saw away to our right, was elevated in thirty-six hours as recently as 1538. Beyond it lies Lake Avernus, — the Tartarus of Virgil. It is all classic soil; and as we came in sight of Baiæ we did not wonder that the Count had been able to make discoveries here, for ivy-draped walls rose on either hand, and we were

GROTTO OF POSILIPPO.

told that from the cliffs ruins of temples, baths, and villas could be seen beneath the water. Nero had a villa here, and used to visit it attended by a thousand carriages and two thousand mules shod with silver, if one may credit the old extravagant traditions. Nat hoped that as an omen of good luck we might find one of the famous silver mule-shoes. Baiæ was the fashionable watering-place, the Newport of Rome also during the time of Augustus and Hadrian.

> "A fair and sumptuous city then stood here,
> Lifting its marble forehead o'er the sea,
> And glittering in the sunny atmosphere
> With calm white masonry."

Horace sang in praise of its gardens; but having gained all this information, it became important to ascertain the situation of the Count's villa. We inquired of an intelligent native, whom we found lounging near the harbor, but he knew nothing of any noble family of the name of Torlonia. This struck us as extremely odd; but we prosecuted our search with diligence, the intelligent native following, apparently much interested in our success.

On the little landing Nat discovered a number of great cases addressed to parties in America. Trying to move them, he was convinced by their weight that they contained statues or fragments of sculpture. The native told us that they were waiting for a bark to convey them to the steamer at Naples. There was a quarry over yonder where they found many of these things. Uncle Jonah was of the opinion that we had chanced upon the antiquity factory, and Nat was wild to visit the quarry at once; but just then a liveried footman appeared, who was profuse with apologies for having missed us, and said that Signor Torlonia had sent him to the inn to watch our coming and to conduct us to the castle. He mounted to the box beside the coachman, and directed him where to drive. As we drove away we saw that the intelligent native had thrust his under lip far out, as it seemed to me in derision. We were taken to a ruinous tower, with a modern addition, very smart and new, springing like an excrescence from its side. On entering this part we found ourselves in a suite of airy rooms sparsely furnished in the Italian style, but adorned with works of art, paintings, busts on pedestals, inlaid cabinets, and other articles of beauty and value. These rooms, although they bore evidence of recent habitation, were quite empty. The servant seemed surprised that his master was not here to receive us, and went in search of him. A curtain veiled a niche or bay-window at the end of the room, and before it on a tripod lay a pillow of flowers, on which the word " Hygeia " was spelled with jasmine blossoms on a background of violets. I could hardly restrain my feminine curiosity until the valet returned, evidently much disappointed that he could not find his master. Victoria laughed. " There is something fatal in my presence," she said; " you will never meet him so long as I am with you."

THE INTELLIGENT NATIVE.

The servant drew aside the curtain to show us the statue which his master considered the gem of his collection. Uncle exclaimed with delight, " No woman's work here ! " and Aunt turned with a triumphant, " Could anything be more beautiful ? Now, Phœbe, you can never compare Calliope Carter's work to this lovely antique ! "

For a moment I was speechless, for the statue, though armless and otherwise mutilated, was certainly most charming, and a sense of failure had taken my breath away ; but at the mention of Calliope Carter's name a sudden conviction came upon me like a flash of lightning. It was Calliope's Hygeia, or a copy of it, artfully disguised it was true, but the design was the same. A similar idea came to Victoria, and Nat related

VIEW OF POZZUOLI.

the circumstance of the first statue having been broken and sold by the stone-cutters to a stranger; but Uncle was very much vexed, and would not be convinced.

" Is it not possible," Victoria asked, " that Mr. Bartlett bought the fragments and disposed of them to the Count ? " This suggestion visibly disturbed Uncle Jonah, and he ordered the coachman to drive us to the quarry of which the native had spoken. The coachman conferred with the Count's servant, who again sprang nimbly to a seat beside him, and brought us to a sort of yard surrounded with open sheds, in which stone-cutters had been employed in " restoring " fragments by cementing heads and bodies together which had probably never before been acquainted, and manufacturing new members where they were needed. I say the men *had been* so engaged, for the establishment was in confusion, and a uniformed government official was reading a document. Nat approached him and endeavored to understand what all the chatter was about. " As nearly as I can make out," he reported, " the authorities have seized Mr. Bartlett's factory, but have not found the scoundrel himself. Perhaps he has gone off in company with the Count."

We returned to Naples rather silent and pensive. Uncle Jonah especially seemed depressed, and when Victoria offered to prescribe for him, was not equal to his customary little joke about fair physicianesses.

If our excursion was partially a failure, we found Mr. Hathaway beaming with delight. " Have you had a pleasant morning ? " I asked.

" Glorious ! " he replied. " The charity schools are doing a most noble work, but there is room for more laborers. One of the most needed teachers has deserted his post through fear of the cholera, and I have thought that possibly as your Italian tour is nearly over I might be spared to take his place."

Uncle looked vexed. " Certainly," he replied, rather tartly. " I

can't see that Nat has improved any faster under your tuition than
with Phœbe, — if she will take him again — " I ran and stopped
Uncle's further speech with a hug.

HAUNTS OF THE CHOLERA.

"But, Mr. Hathaway," I said, "we are really sorry to have you
leave our party ; must you do so ? "

"I think the duty is plain," he replied ; "the cholera is here, and
there will be a panic."

TEMPLE OF DIANA AT BAIÆ.

"The cholera is here!" shrieked Aunt Pen; "then we must leave Naples at once."

"It is confined to the poorest parts of the city," Mr. Hathaway replied, "and there is no danger for people who live properly."

Victoria helped to pacify Aunt Pen, and she decided to delay her departure for a day or two, as she wished to make some purchases, — a set of Neapolitan coral and some lava ornaments.

I went out with Victoria in the afternoon. "I am going to take some medicines to the poor people," she said; "perhaps you had better not go with me."

"I would like to do so if there is no danger," I replied. "I will stay outside where people are really sick, but I want to see how the poor live here."

It was a sad pilgrimage, for the people were so ungrateful. They met Victoria's kindness with scowls and mutterings. Some refused to take her gifts, or threw them into the street after her. Only the little children were thankful, and to them she explained what to do if any one was stricken with the dread disease. When we returned to the hotel, I gave my dress to Victoria to be disinfected. "You must not go with me again," she said, "for there is enough danger to warrant your uncle and aunt in their apprehensions. They will probably leave Naples with you to-morrow, but I must stay here. I think these poor people need me even more than you do."

"But, Victoria, they will not let you stay at the hotel, and go back and forward among the sick."

"Then I will open a little dispensary somewhere among the poor."

"Oh, Victoria," I cried, "you must not. You will die."

"No, indeed," she replied cheerfully, "I know how to take every precaution. In times like this fear makes more victims than the cholera; and I am not in the least afraid."

While we were chatting, a card was handed me. It was the Count! "Come down too, Victoria," I exclaimed; "at last you shall see him."

" I will follow," she said, "since your aunt has not come in, and you desire it."

I found the Count pacing the parlor in some agitation, with his watch in his hand. He began speaking rapidly. " I was suddenly called away this morning on vitally important business. I had not even time to leave an apology with my servants; but I received the note which you left for me, and I have kept your appointment, though at much inconvenience to myself and some possible risk. A steamer in which I have taken passage sails in half an hour. I have a great deal to say to you, and must do it in few words."

" But, Count Torlonia, I did not make any appointment, or write you any note."

The window-curtain behind me was thrown back, and our ghost, the photographer, sprang into the room. " No, Miss," he said, while from the opposite door two officers entered and seized the Count's arms; " it was I who took the liberty to write the note. I have been making pretty careful observations as to the habits of this individual, and when he gave me the slip at Baiæ, I calculated that a letter from you would make him show himself as quickly as anything."

The Count looked very defiant, as he said haughtily, " You shall pay for this violence to an Italian nobleman ! " But at that instant Victoria entered the room, and fixed her calm, questioning gaze upon him. The man's demeanor changed instantly. He seemed to shrink into insignificance. Victoria, on the contrary, seemed to grow taller as she exclaimed, " Senhor Silva — Mr. Bartlett! is this you ? "

" Yes, Miss Delavan," replied the photographer, "this is the original sarpent; and I 'm happy to have you here to identify him, and to witness the fact that Detective Jenkins is not to be fooled every time."

So this is the end. The Count is an impostor who would have been unmasked long ago if Victoria had seen him. Uncle says that Calliope shall have an extra five hundred since her work is so good that it could be mistaken for the antique; and since the mutilated statue is so lovely, he is quite ready to believe that the perfect one is much more so. We start for Sicily to-morrow, and thence to America, when I hope to complete my course at Vassar. Even Aunt makes no objection. If Vassar helped in the making of such a young woman as Victoria, she is quite willing to have me receive its impress.

As for me, I have learned that many qualifications which I had not suspected are necessary for the successful following of the career of a society woman; and not least important in the list, I am sure, are a thorough education and wide culture, a steady courage and a generous heart.

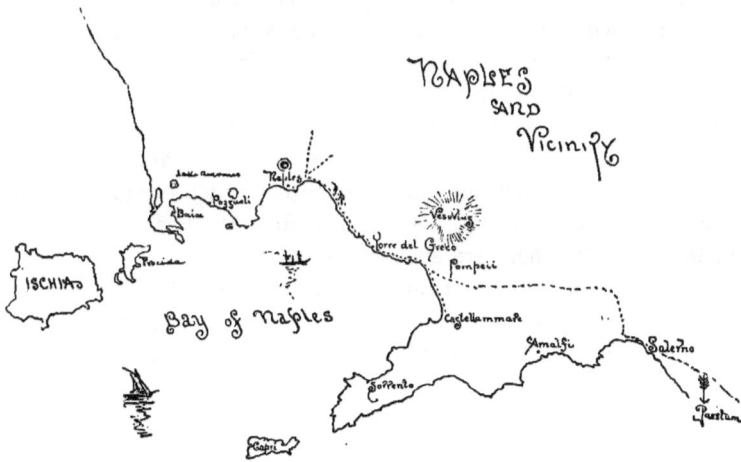

CHAPTER XIV.

SICILY.

I REMEMBER as a child how Sicily looked to me upon the map, — a misshapen animal, which the toe of the Italian boot was always ready to spurn. Since that time I have read and heard little of Sicily, and I do not think I would have cared greatly beforehand to make this postscript to our Italian tour, if Uncle had not decided that the most convenient way to return to America would be by one of the Vincenzo Florio steamers, which ply between Palermo and New York.

What is my surprise, therefore, to find that this Sicilian postscript contains, as that part of a woman's letter is said to do, the most interesting part of the whole epistle.

Uncle sent a check to Calliope, from Naples, with directions as to how and where to have the statue sent; and then we bade good-by to Victoria and Mr. Hathaway. It has seemed strange to me since, that we felt no pang of compunction at leaving Victoria in such an unprotected way in a strange and plague-stricken city. On the contrary, all of us felt that we were a party of children venturing away without our natural guardian and protector. I shall never be so self-reliant, no, not if I live to a hundred years; but I am thankful that there are such women.

We came by way of the Lipari Isles and stopped at Lipari, first passing the volcanic island of Stromboli. It is a huge cone rising out of the sea, said to be very difficult of ascent. Lipari is formed

of scoria, and has a grim, forbidding look, as though its hidden
fires might at any instant belch forth, and the lava engulf the old
town, which slumbers picturesquely at the foot of a volcanic cone.
We did not have time to ascend to the summit of the volcano,
but we bought some beautiful specimens of pink and yellow sub-
limates of sulphur, and visited the castle where brigands are confined. We heard one of them singing — what but " Dolce Napoli,"
the very song that our handsome guide at Capri had trolled forth
so lustily? —

> "O dolce Napoli;
> O suol beato,
> Ove sorridere
> Volleil creato;
> Tu sei l' impero,
> Dell' armoria !
> Santa Lucia !
> Santa Lucia ! "

Was he from Naples, we wondered, or from Capri, — this brigand
with the languishing eyes, and small gold ear-rings half hidden in
his curly hair? There was a medal on his breast, Santa Lucia or
the Virgin, and there were poniard scars beneath it, we were told,
given by the soldiers who effected his capture, but not until he had
killed three of their number and dangerously wounded two others, —
this gentle brigand with the entrancing tenor voice. Seeing that
we were interested in the prisoners, the jailer explained, through
our guide, that there was an American confined there, who had
recently been arrested in Naples for fraudulently representing himself to be an Italian nobleman. There were other charges against him
in America, where he would eventually be transported, but the Italian
Government desired to settle its little grievance with him first.
Perhaps we would like to see him, — he was a distinguished-looking
man. But with one voice we decided that we did not wish to see
this interesting convict. It was in the crater of an extinct volcano

in South America that Victoria first became convinced of his per-
fidy, and this seems a very appropriate place to leave him.

Palermo soon lay before us, its white walls glancing in the sunshine between the forest of masts in the harbor and the gray mass

THE FILLE-DE-CHAMBRE.

of Pellegrino in the distance. We walked
up the long quay to the hotel, and it
seemed to us that the city had a semi-
Oriental look, to which it has a perfect
right, as the Saracens had much to do
with its architecture. The hotel is quite
cosmopolitan; has an Algerine cook, a
Spanish head-waiter, and a pretty French
fille-de-chambre, who wears bewitching caps
and aprons, and spends her time on the
balconies with a feather duster ostenta-
tiously displayed, — apparently her insignia of office, for I have never seen her
use it.

Society in Palermo is said to be very
pleasant. There are numerous English
residents, and we have already received
calls from the American consul and his
wife, and from the rector of the Episco-
pal Church. Then we are making agreeable acquaintances in the
house. The surly old English officer with his startled daughter,
whom we noticed at Rome, are here. He is waiting for the arrival
of a British man-of-war now at Gibraltar, and will then leave the
young girl with friends here, and depart for the seat of war, where-
ever that may be. Strange to say, we have just met a young
American, the Dr. Stillman of whom Victoria spoke to us, who is
also waiting for the man-of-war, as he expects to join the expedition
as surgeon. It was by the merest chance that we happened to be

PALERMO AND MOUNT PELLIGRINO.

MONREALE.

introduced, and all through the old officer whom we had voted so disagreeable. I told him about Victoria's decision to stay and care for the poor people in Naples; but he did not seem in the least surprised, and I thought he undervalued the action. "Was it not a remarkable, a really wonderful thing to do?" I asked.

"No," he replied, "not for her. It is only just what I should have expected."

Then for an instant he looked at me, and I saw by an indescribable expression in his quiet eyes that he appreciates Victoria as fully as I do, and perhaps loves her more. I wonder what may have come between these two.

We have visited the cathedral and other places of interest in the city, and have just returned from a long-to-be-remembered drive to Monreale, a picturesque town on the heights of Monte Caputo, not far from Palermo. On our way we passed the picturesque village of Bocca di Falco, and a wild gorge which leads to the convent of San Martino, then by beautiful villas and through a shady glen, up, up the mountain with whitey-gray olive-trees, cacti, aloes in long procession carrying their tall blossom-shafts like branched candlesticks borne aslant, orange and almond trees, bougainevilleas, and oleanders, on every hand, making an Eden of the mountain-slope. We had come to see the cathedral; but the ride itself was its own recompense, though the building, with its mingling of Norman and Greek styles, is especially interesting. The elaborately ornamented archway over the west gate, with its rich mosaics, and carvings representing knights in battle and grotesque beasts intricately joined by graceful foliations, was a study in architecture. Altogether it was a perfect day, and one that we shall never forget. If Mr. Hathaway had been with us, he would have given us the history of the entire island, with a special dissertation on the Sicilian Vespers. Instead of this, Dr. Stillman read George Eliot's poem of Sicily, — "How Lisa Loved the King."

THE CUB.

I wish I might see more of the island. It would be a charming plan to make a cruise around it in a yacht, stopping at Messina, Syracuse, and other interesting points, with a donkey-trip to Mount Ætna; but possibly Scylla and Charybdis might not be favorable to the plan.

Day after to-morrow is my birthday, and I am to have a little company. We have become acquainted with several people, and Aunt Pen says I may invite them all to a little fete in our rooms. It will be a rather heterogeneous company, for the people are not all from the same ranks of society. There is one English boy here with his tutor, whom Nat calls the Cub. He affects great carelessness in his dress, and what he supposes are "Americanisms" in language, though such very stupid slang I never heard in America. I am almost afraid to include him in my list, for I fear he will disgrace us; but I am confident that he needs a glimpse of good society. Then there is a sweet girl who has a wonderful voice and is to be a public singer. I think the stricter people look at her askance; but it seems to me that is just the way to drive her into more questionable company, and that she needs our support and encouragement, for good and gentle she certainly is. We have, too, a sallow old gentleman who is very rich and very solitary, troubled with a fortune that he does not know what to do with, and a complaint of the liver. I shall invite him, though I don't believe he will come. I wish Americans would pay more attention to

THE SOLITARY GENTLEMAN.

decorum while abroad. The Cub told Nat that he liked Americans because they were so jolly unconventional. He met a party of them at Smyrna, and the young ladies walked along the principal promenade with fez caps on their heads.

The Cub came to breakfast wearing a rubber overcoat, and Aunt Pen was so indignant that she would not recognize him. I think he was rather ashamed of himself, and I have noticed since that he tries to copy Nat's neckties.

Besides the people I have mentioned, who interest me, Aunt Pen thinks, simply because other people would find them uninteresting, I am to have some titled personages, — a pretty marchioness who wears impossible hats, especially arranged, Nat says, to accommodate her coronet inside ; and a member of the Royal Academy, who is the lion of all assemblages. The entertainment has been left entirely to me, and I have my ideas.

The New York steamer has just arrived. I shall only have time for my birthday party, and then we take passage for home. Among the passengers who have come out on the steamer is, strange to say, Victoria's father, Mr. Delavan. As soon as he heard that we were going to Naples, he became alarmed and started for Italy. At least, this is my interpretation of his conduct, though he says he had thought previously of joining his daughter this summer.

My fete has proved a surprise-party indeed. The solitary gentleman did come, and sent me in advance a basket of exquisite flowers. The Cub appeared with his bristling hair nicely cut, and his awkward hands squeezed

THE MARCHIONESS.

into new gloves. I had asked our musical friend to sing for me ; and she sang " Flee as a Bird," and "Consider the Lilies," so simply and sweetly that every one was delighted. I saw the Marchioness talking with her afterward, and there were tears in her noble eyes. Dr. Stillman read for us again. This time he chose " The Sicilian's Tale," from Longfellow's " Wayside Inn."

Afterward Mr. Delavan came and chatted with me as he sipped an ice. " Every one says this is one of the most charming evenings he has ever enjoyed," he said; "but I think I am the only one who has discovered that the character of the evening has been distinctly religious."

"Then you have penetrated Phœbe's little scheme," Nat replied. "She wanted to see if she could make these people enjoy a prayer-meeting without knowing it."

"Not quite a prayer-meeting," I explained; "but I do think our social enjoyment may be of a higher order than it often is."

"That is just like Victoria," said Dr. Stillman. Mr. Delavan started, and scrutinized the young man; whereupon I introduced him, and Mr. Delavan said, "Excuse my brusqueness; I thought at first you were speaking of my daughter." Then I explained the situation, and the two were soon talking so earnestly that I was quite forgotten. Shortly after this we were startled by a loud knock; the door was flung open, and Mr. Hathaway stood with his hand upon the knob, but so aged and changed that we scarcely knew him. Aunt Pen threw up her hands in dismay.

"MR. HATHAWAY STOOD WITH HIS HAND UPON THE KNOB."

"You bring bad news!" she exclaimed. "Some one is dead!"

"I trust not," he replied gravely, "but Victoria is very ill."

Then there was consternation and confusion. I wanted to go to her at once, but Mr. Delavan would not allow it.

"It is cholera, child," he said sternly, "and you would be running a great risk where you can do no good. It is fortunate that I am here. I will take Dr. Stillman with me, and we shall be enough; for Mr. Hathaway tells me that she has a devoted nurse in the person of an Italian woman whom she has bene-fited. We will do all that can be done. If we were only there at this moment! Mr. Hathaway came in one of those lateen-sailed feluccas, and the regular steamer will not leave until to-morrow afternoon." ·

It was then that the Cub came to the rescue like an angel of light. "Lord Luffaway has left his steam-yacht with me for a week, and I'll take you across," he said; "I'd like nothing better."

And so they have gone, and I stand aloof from my dearest friend, bound hand and foot by Aunt and Uncle, who will not let me go. It is wicked, cruel; and if I were only of age this birthday I would openly revolt. Dr. Stillman has de-

"AUNT PEN THREW UP HER HANDS IN DISMAY."

clined the position which he had thought so advantageous and which was just within his grasp. The British officer went away from the party grumbling like a tolerably active volcano, and charging him with fickleness and indifference to his own interests. If he had but known it was faithfulness instead, and regard for dearer interests than mere posi-tion! Oh, I cannot leave her so! I must make one last appeal.

I have been successful, and we return to Naples by the regular boat to-morrow, — Uncle and I. Aunt will remain here with Nat, awaiting the result. I am all impatience to be off, and tremble lest I may be too late.

NAPLES AGAIN.

I have seen Victoria. They say she is better, in fact, out of
danger, but she was sadly changed, — so pale and quiet; but there
was a heavenly joy and peace in her face instead of the old animation.
Her father led me to her bedside, where Dr. Stillman sat holding her
white hand, though I do not think he was feeling her pulse. For
a moment it seemed to me that I was punished for my half-desertion,
and that she really did not need me; but she turned to me quickly,
with her old look of interest, and exclaimed, " Why, Phœbe, child !
I thought you were on your way to America."

I do not remember what I said, only that I cried and laughed
until Dr. Stillman told me that I would excite her; and then I became calm for fear of being banished, and had the satisfaction of
seeing that she was glad of my coming. She called me, mistakenly
enough, a heroine, and said I had braved death for her sake. But
they would not let me stay and nurse her, for of that there is no
need, and as soon as she is able to bear the ride, she is to be taken
to Sorrento, to recover in a villa that overlooks the gorge where
Agnes lived. If it were not that I am sure she is happier in the
thought that I did not desert, I should think my return an unneces-
sary one; but I know that my love is dear to her, eclipsed though
it may well be by the greater one which now broods over her.
For Victoria and Dr. Stillman understand each other at last,
and are to be married some time, though not, she insists, until
she has finished her medical course and obtained her degree. This
possibly accounts for the absurd happiness which beams in both
their faces and is reflected in a lesser degree from that of Mr.
Delavan.

After all, I cannot flatter myself that I should have been greatly
missed if I had gone on to America; but I could not have borne the

dreadful uncertainty, and to see her so nearly well and so perfectly happy is worth a far longer journey.

And now we hurry back to Aunt Pen, who is doubtless consumed with anxiety on my account, and then away over the broad Atlantic

"UNDER NEW ENGLAND APPLE-TREES."

to a certain home under New England apple-trees, where I shall look over broad meadows, and nestle down in the clover and kiss the very ground for delight; for better than Italy, better than any other land, is one's own dear home!

SWITZERLAND

Geneva

L. Lugano

L. Como

L. Garda

Mt. Cenis

Turin

Milan

Verona

Padua

AUSTRIA

Venice

Ferrara

Genoa

Bologna

Dalmatia

Pisa

Florence

Leghorn

ITALY

Corsica

Tyrhenian Sea

Adriatic

Rome

Sea

Naples

Mt. Vesuvius
Pompeii

Capri

SARDINIA

MEDITERRANEAN

SICILY

AFRICA

SEA

Malta

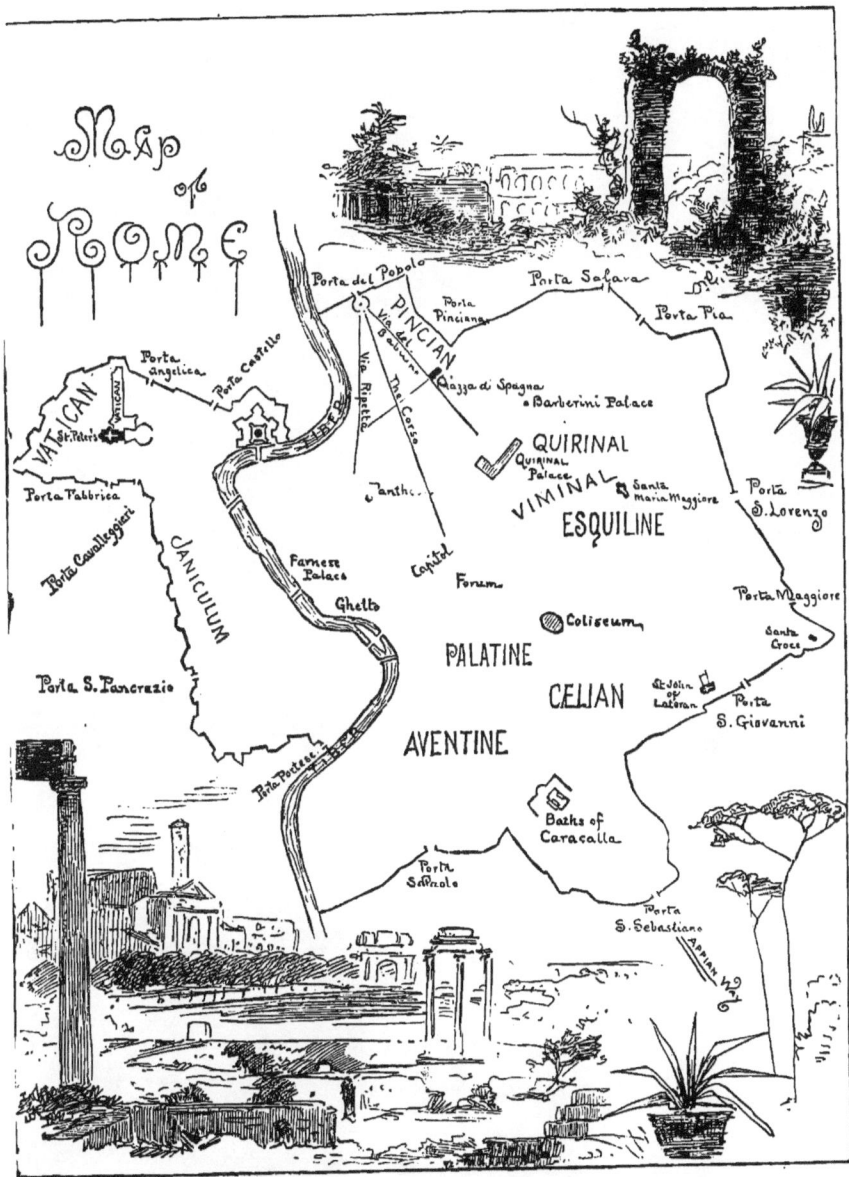

Map of Rome

VATICAN
St. Peter's
Porta Angelica
Porta Castello
Porta Fabbrica
Porta Cavalleggieri

JANICULUM
Porta S. Pancrazio

Porta del Popolo
Porta Pinciana
PINCIAN
Via del Babuino
Via Ripetta
The Corso
Piazza di Spagna
Barberini Palace
QUIRINAL
Quirinal Palace
VIMINAL
Santa Maria Maggiore
ESQUILINE

Porta Salara
Porta Pia
Porta S. Lorenzo

Pantheon
Capitol
Forum
Farnese Palace
Ghetto

Porta Maggiore
Santa Croce

PALATINE
Coliseum
CELIAN
St. John of Lateran
Porta S. Giovanni

AVENTINE
Porta Portese
Baths of Caracalla

Porta S. Paolo
Porta S. Sebastiano
Appian Way

www.ingramcontent.com/pod-product-compliance
Lightning Source LLC
Chambersburg PA
CBHW030404270326
41926CB00009B/1264